Collins *gem*

Whisky

D0191383

Carol P. Shaw

HarperCollins*Publishers*
Westerhill Road, Bishopbriggs, Glasgow G64 2QT

www.collins.co.uk

First published 1993
Third edition published 1999
This edition published 2004

Reprint 10 9 8 7 6 5 4 3 2

ISBN 0-00-7144113

The author and publishers would like to thank all the distillers,
independent bottlers and trade associations who kindly assisted
in the preparation of information and material for this book.

Typeset by Davidson Pre-Press Graphics Limited, Glasgow.

Printed in Italy by Amadeus S.r.l.

CONTENTS

The Whiskies of Scotland 63

Taste Rating 64

INTRODUCTION

Welcome to the fourth edition of Collins *Gem Whisky*. A review of the years since the first edition (published in 1993) shows an industry that has faced a series of constant challenges: governments perceived to view whisky as an all-too-easy source of revenue; competition from a whole new brand of increasingly outlandish spirit-and-mixer drinks; and consolidation and rationalization of the industry by remote, multi-national companies with headquarters hundreds or even thousands of miles away.

A look behind these first impressions reveals a slightly different picture. Duty on a bottle of whisky, while still hefty by European standards, remains the same today as it was in 1993 – due certainly to vociferous and active lobbying by the Scotch Whisky Association, and possibly at least in part to a Chancellor mindful of both the importance of the industry to the UK, and the right of everyone to enjoy its product.

And after a short period of experimentation in the best ways to meet competition from the new generation of pre-mixed drinks (Bells and Bru, anyone?), the advantages of trading on whisky's natural advantages, notably its superior quality, were quicky realised.

Consolidation there has certainly been, and the swallowing up of smaller operations by bigger fish. Yet an interesting and very welcome spin-off from such take-overs and mergers has been, ironically, a fragmentation and reinvigoration in some areas. Fresh-thinking Inver House Distillers were able to buy five distilleries, re-energizing their product and watching sales rise in the process. And new distilleries are starting: Isle of Arran began bottling in the '90s, and today new distilleries are planned, from Campbeltown, once the home of whisky in the south-west, to the proposed Blackwood Distillery near Lerwick.

Others such as Bruichladdich, Bladnoch, Edradour and Tullibardine have been bought individually – often by bottlers but always by enthusiasts – and their new owners have brought not just fresh thinking but a new lease of life to distilleries that might otherwise have stayed silent. They have also been quick to catch on to the benefits of direct marketing via the internet – one look at the websites of Bruichladdich or Edradour shows how much creativity goes into their marketing. The web has also been used to great effect by dynamic small firms like Loch Fyne Whiskies.

But creativity isn't just the preserve of small, dedicated outfits. Bacardi-owned Dewar's brand opened the interactive World of Whisky visitor attraction at Aberfeldy Distillery, doing an admirable job of demystifying and entertaining at the same time. The Famous Grouse Experience, at Glenturret, has been the latest to follow this trend.

And if the proof of the whisky is in the drinking, sales figures for the first part of 2003, up 50% on the same period in 2002, suggest that the whisky industry is definitely doing something right. Overall, on Collins *Gem Whisky*'s tenth birthday, it's fair to say that things in the twenty-first century are in a better shape than they were at the end of the twentieth. Long may the fusion of innovation and tradition continue.

Slàinte mhath!

THE HISTORY OF SCOTCH WHISKY-MAKING

It is widely accepted that whisky has been distilled in Scotland for hundreds of years, and different hypotheses as to its origins have been suggested. Some state that it was brought into the country by missionary monks from Ireland; others point out that, as the Arabs were among the first to learn distillation techniques, knights and men returning from the Crusades could have brought the knowledge back with them. It may well be, however, that it evolved simply as a means of using up barley which would otherwise have been ruined after a wet harvest.

A good supply of water is a prerequisite for distilling

The name itself is derived from the Gaelic, *uisge beatha*, meaning 'water of life'. The Latin equivalent, *aqua vitae*, was a term which was commonly used throughout Europe to describe the local spirit. *Aqua vitae* made its first appearance in official Scottish records in 1494, with the record of malt being sold to one Friar John Cor with which to make the malt, but *uisge* seems to have first been mentioned in the account of the funeral and wake of

a Highland chieftain around 1618. The amount of whisky-making throughout Scotland increased greatly during the seventeenth century, and nowhere more so than in the Highlands. In fact, so enthusiastic was the growth in distillation that before the end of the sixteenth century there had already been complaints in Parliament that so much barley was being used in whisky production that it was in short supply as a foodstuff! These distillers' method was basic and simple: a sack of barley might be soaked in water – for example, in a burn – for a day or two, then the barley would be spread out in a dry place, allowing it to sprout, for around 10 days. The sprouting would be halted by drying the

history of Scotch

barley over a peat fire (peat being used as the main source of fuel in the Highlands). It was then put in a container with boiling water and yeast, to ferment. This mix would be passed twice through a pot still, emerging as whisky at the other end. These distillers had to be fairly skilled at their job, to possess the judgement to know when to take off the middle cut of the spirit (the drinkable part), avoiding the poisonous foreshots, at the start of the distillation, and the lower-quality feints, or aftershots, at the end. Although they had no instruments, methods did evolve of testing the whisky's strength, including setting fire to the spirit to measure the amount of liquid left behind, and mixing it with gunpowder to see how it reacted when ignited – if the gunpowder-and-whisky cocktail exploded, it was known that the whisky was too strong!

It was during the seventeenth century, too, that the first tax on whisky was introduced by Parliament, because of the pressing need to raise revenue to finance the army fighting in the British Civil War in 1644. Although it was reduced under the Commonwealth, this episode effectively marked the beginning of the principle of the taxation of whisky.

The union of Scotland and England in 1707, however, heralded some changes for the whisky industry, and few of them were constructive. A malt tax was introduced in 1725 which adversely affected the quality of beer – until then the most popular drink – and of whiskies produced by the professional commercial distillers in the more populous Lowlands, who were obliged to produce whiskies of poorer quality, with less malted barley content. These taxes also applied to Highland malt whisky, but in that

Opposite: a page from an eighteenth-century guide to distilling, showing how little the design of the basic equipment has changed

still-inaccessible region it was much easier to ignore, and illicit distillation continued to flourish. This attempt at revenue raising, affecting the Lowland distillers but ignored in the Highlands, set a pattern for the rest of the century.

The large distillers in the Lowlands continued successfully to produce rough grain whisky, whose quantity was more important than its quality, for consumption locally and in England where it was often used as a basis for cheap gin. However, pressure from the English distillers, who were being undercut by Scottish imports flooding the market, encouraged Parliament to introduce a series of increasingly draconian taxes against the Scots whisky. The small distillers in the Highlands – most of whom were probably farmers and crofters, pursuing a lucrative sideline – continued to make superior quality whisky without paying tax. Much of this whisky was brought to the Lowlands for sale, where it was more popular with those who could afford it than the rougher spirit produced by the Lowland distillers. The government in London had no answer to the problems they had helped create in the whisky industry, other than to raise taxes still further, making the law seem more and more ineffectual.

Finally, however, pressure on the government brought an abandonment of its futile attempts at taxation and regulation. A Royal Commission was set up to investigate the industry, the Excise service in the Highlands was strengthened, and in 1822

history of Scotch

A The Still	L A Pewter Crane
B The Worm tub	M A Pewter Valentia
C The Pump	N Hippocrates bag or Flannel
D Water tub	Sleeve
E A Press	O Poker Fire-shovel Cole rake
FFF Tubs to hold the goods	P A Box of Bungs
GGGG Canns of different size	Q The Worm within the Worm tub
H A Wood Funnel with a iron nosel	markd with prick'd lines
I A large Vessel to put the Feuns	R A Piece of Wood to keep down
or after runnings	the Head of the Still to
K Tin pump	prevent flying of

Sir Edward Landseer's somewhat romanticized depiction of an illicit still in the Highlands (Diageo)

an act was passed which brought harsher penalties for those found to be operating unlicensed stills. The following year the Excise Act made an attempt to encourage licensed distilling, cutting both duty and restrictions on exports to England. Now, an annual licence of £10 was introduced on stills over forty gallons (smaller stills were not allowed), and a more modest duty of 2/3d per gallon of whisky brought in. The Duke of Gordon, whose estates included the Glenlivet area, was a prime mover in the reforms, and he encouraged his tenants, including George Smith, producer of the whisky which came to be known as The Glenlivet, to take out

history of Scotch

licences. The new act was effective and successful, and the amount of legally distilled whisky consumed had risen threefold by 1827.

Freed from its legislative shackles, the whisky industry was able to concentrate on the development of its product and markets. The product itself was given an impetus by the invention by Aeneas Coffey, an Irish former exciseman, of a new still which he patented in 1832; this allowed the distillation of grain whisky to take place in a continuous process in one still. The new process cut back on costs, allowing the Lowland grain distillers to use even less malted barley than before, and to produce on an even bigger scale. Ironically, however, the success of the Excise Act and the new patent still brought trouble for the industry during the mid-nineteenth century, because of overproduction and despite the exploiting of new export markets in the Empire and overseas. This development saw the foreshadowing of the emergence of the Distillers Company, with the six biggest Lowland grain whisky producers combining in a price-fixing cartel; they were not to join together officially, however, until 1877, by which time the face of the industry had changed dramatically.

This change was brought about by the development of techniques of blending malt and grain whiskies to produce a lighter spirit than the traditional single malt, and a more flavoursome one than grain whisky. In the 1850s Andrew Usher, the Edinburgh whisky merchant who was agent for the Glenlivet whiskies, had vatted together several casks of Glenlivet from his stocks, producing in the process a much more consistent product. The practice was soon extended to the blending of malt and grain. This was held to produce a lighter spirit which English drinkers, unused to the much stronger malt product of the pot still, found much more palatable. It also introduced an element of consistency to the product. Coincidentally, this development came when reserves of brandy, the first-choice spirit in England, were threatened as a result of the Phylloxera blight in the French vineyards in the 1860s. Timely exploitation of the market in England by the grain producers and blenders meant that, as stocks of brandy declined in the 1870s and '80s, the new blended whiskies came to take their place as the quality spirit, and the 1890s was a period of unprecedented growth for the Scottish whisky industry. New malt distilleries were opened and groups like Distillers and the North British Distillery Company, serving the interests of the grain distillers and the blenders respectively, became phenomenally successful. The whisky industry was developing to become recognizable as the industry it is today.

One of Andrew Usher's blends

The boom period was followed, typically, by a slump, and difficult times for the industry at the beginning of this century were compounded by the First World War and the introduction of Prohibition in the USA in 1920. The years from then to the Second World War saw a drop in output of almost 50%, and an almost complete halt being brought to the production of malt whisky.

This situation continued after the war when, naturally, what grain was available had to be diverted to feed the people rather than make whisky. As prosperity returned in the 1950s, whisky output increased and exports rose. New distilleries were built in the 1960s, old ones reopened, and the production of malt whisky quadrupled in a decade. Take-over and consolidation were the keynotes of the industry in the 1970s, with English brewers moving into the whisky market on a large scale. This trend culminated in the messy take-over of the Distillers Company (now United Distillers) by Guinness, a transaction which resulted in the chairman of the brewing giant and several of his advisers ending up in court. Ironically, however, the adage of there being no bad publicity seems to be borne out by the Distillers take-over: an episode which apparently brought the industry into disrepute, came at a time when the market was picking up again after the slump lasting from the mid '70s to the mid '80s, and served to give whisky a timely publicity boost.

This upturn in the drink's fortunes continued into the 1990s, with the emphasis in marketing being placed on quality rather than quantity: cheaper blends have tended to disappear, single malts are taking an increasing share of the market, and price rises are being met by consumers, who seem to prefer the new expensive-and-exclusive image of the drink. Increasing importance was placed on packaging and advertising, and with the marketing of new visitor centres in the distilleries themselves as tourist attractions in their own right. By 1995, however, growth in the Scotch market as a whole had slowed once again and the industry was having to work hard to maintain its position. The premium

Lochranza Distillery on the Isle of Arran. Opened in 1995, it is one of Scotland's newest distilleries (Isle of Arran Distilleries Ltd)

end of the industry continued to be healthy (helped no doubt by the first reduction in excise duty for a hundred years) although the mass-market sector faced increasing competition, particularly from vodka producers. It responded by the creation of whisky-based drinks designed to appeal to a younger, less traditional customer base – whiskies spiked with red chilli peppers, for example – but by 1998 the producing companies had largely decided to abandon such experiments. Instead, it turned to television advertising in an attempt to woo younger consumers in both the UK and the USA. The full impact of such TV advertising may not be seen for several years.

More heartening is the way the drinks industry has performed in the years since the abandonment of the European Union's popular duty-free scheme, and the consequent loss of a market worth up to £80 million to Scotch producers. In response to this challenge,

history of Scotch

and to tough competition in the global market as a whole, the whisky industry has held its own in established areas such as Europe and North America, and has begun to make inroads into the new and potentially lucrative markets of eastern Europe and southeast Asia.

The late 1990s and early years of the new century were also marked by a trend for rationalization and consolidation among the major drinks manufacturers. They closed a number of distilleries or sold them on, often to independent bottlers, which is surely a good indicator of the growing vigour of the market for more exclusive single malts.

There were also a number of major corporate realignments in this period, the most prominent being the £27 billion merger of Guinness (United Distillers) and Grand Metropolitan in 1997 to create Diageo, the largest drinks company in the world. In 2001, Scotland's biggest ever management buy-out took place, allowing the creation of Whyte & MacKay Ltd.

As the new century begins, the industry appears in robust good health: 90% of whisky is exported and malt whisky exports are up almost 50%. Meanwhile, several new distilleries are being planned including one in Shetland which is due to be built in 2004.

The industry has a history of facing crises and challenges, and emerging strongly from them – a pattern which seems set to continue, and something which can only be good for all those who appreciate and love good whisky.

HOW SCOTCH WHISKY IS MADE

Two different processes are used for the distillation of Scotch malt and grain whiskies.

MALT WHISKY

In malt whisky distillation, there are several basic steps to the process: malting, mashing, fermentation, distillation and maturation, although the minor elements may vary from one distillery to another. Barley may be bought in pre-malted, but if it is not, it is first filtered to remove any foreign matter.

Malted barley

Malting

The process begins when the barley is transferred to soak in tanks of water which go by the self-explanatory name of barley steeps; this process takes two to four days. In the traditional process, the barley is then spread on a malting floor, to be turned by hand daily for the next twelve days or so, allowing it to sprout; now, however, most distilleries use mechanical devices for turning the sprouting barley. As the seeds germinate, the starch in the barley releases some of its sugars. At the appropriate moment, germination is stopped by drying the cereal in a malt kiln over a peat furnace or fire. The peat smoke which flavours the drying barley at this stage can, depending on its intensity, be tasted in the final whisky itself.

Turning the barley by hand on a traditional malting floor

how Scotch is made

Top: adding peat to the kiln

Bottom: a traditional pagoda-topped malting kiln

how Scotch is made

The malt kilns traditionally had the pagoda-style roofs which were such an instantly recognizable characteristic of the malt distilleries; these can still be seen on older distilleries.

Mashing

The next stage for the malted barley is passage through a mill, from which it emerges roughly ground as grist. From here it is moved to a mash tun, a large vat where it is mixed with hot water and agitated, so that its sugars dissolve to produce wort, a sweet, non-alcoholic liquid. This process is repeated to ensure that all the sugars have been collected. The solid remains of the barley are removed at this point for conversion to cattle food.

Inside the mash tun and (inset) the worts it produces

Traditional and modern washbacks

how Scotch is made

Fermentation

The wort is cooled and transferred to washbacks, large vats where yeast is added and the process of fermentation begins. The chemical reaction which takes place with the addition of the yeast converts the sugars in the wort to alcohol, a process which takes around two days and results in a low-strength alcoholic liquid now called wash.

Distillation

The wash is then ready for the stills. The shape of the still is one of the most important factors in the whisky-making process, as it can have a decisive influence on the final character of the malt whisky:

for instance, a still with a short neck will produce a whisky with heavier oils and a more intense flavour, whereas lighter-flavoured whiskies with less heavy oils will emerge from a still with a long or high neck. The first still which the wash passes through is known, appropriately, as the wash still, and here it is heated. As the alcohol has a lower boiling point than water, the alcoholic steam rises up the still through its long spout to the worm,

How Scotch malt whisky is made

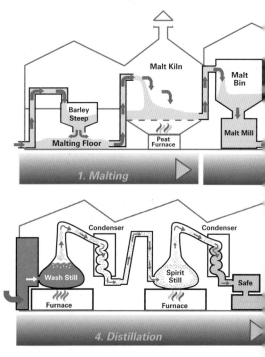

Malt Kiln

Malt Bin

Barley Steep

Malting Floor

Peat Furnace

Malt Mill

1. Malting

Condenser

Condenser

Wash Still

Spirit Still

Safe

Furnace

Furnace

4. Distillation

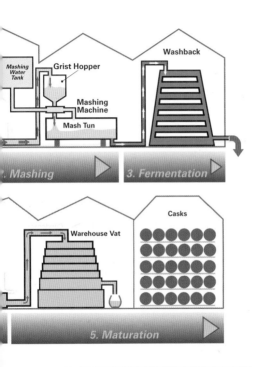

Mashing Water Tank

Grist Hopper

Mashing Machine

Mash Tun

Washback

2. Mashing ▷

3. Fermentation ▷

Warehouse Vat

Casks

5. Maturation ▷

how Scotch is made

a condensing coil. The distillate, now called low wines, is passed into the second still, the spirit still, where the process is repeated, with the liquid running off into the glass-fronted spirit safe.

Drawing off a sample of the new whisky in the spirit safe

It is at this point that the skill of the distiller is crucial: unable to smell or taste the liquid to judge it, he must know when to separate the middle cut, or main run of the spirit, which contains the best-quality alcohol needed for malt whisky, from the foreshots (the raw, poisonous first distillate) and the feints, or aftershots, which contain a lower grade of alcohol. Once separated, foreshots and feints are fed back into the wash for redistillation.

Maturation

The main run of the alcohol is now transferred for storage to a vat and is mixed with water to bring it down in strength.

how Scotch is made

It is then transferred into casks for maturing. The whole process of distillation can theoretically be completed inside a week, but the whisky must now mature for at least three years before it can be sold; during this time, a small percentage of the whisky, known as the 'angels' share', will evaporate. In practice, malt whiskies are left to mature for an average of eight to fifteen years.

GRAIN WHISKY

With the exception of the Invergordon Distillery, grain distilleries have traditionally been located in the Lowlands. Grain distilleries use patent (or Coffey) stills, which can operate continuously. The basic process used is similar to that for malt, up to the point of distillation, although everything takes place on a much larger scale, and with much less malted barley: maize, unmalted barley or other cereals are more commonly used.

Distillation is carried out in two large cylindrical columns which are linked by pipes. The wash passes into the first column, the rectifier, in a coiled pipe running through its length. Jets of steam are forced up into the column, through a series of perforated plates between which the coiled pipe passes, heating the wash inside before it passes out and into the analyser. In the analyser the wash is no longer in the coiled pipe, and it is now met by another jet of steam passing through more perforated plates. The steam and evaporated alcohol rise and are passed back into the rectifier, with the alcohol cooling as it moves up, encountering fresh, cold wash in the coiled pipe on its way down, until it reaches a cold water coil where it condenses before passing out of the still. The impure alcohols in the first and last part of the distillate can be redistilled, while the alcohol which reaches the spirit safe and receiver is very pure. The whisky will mature faster than malt, and is less subject to variable factors. The vast majority of the produce will go for blending not long after its three-year maturation period has passed.

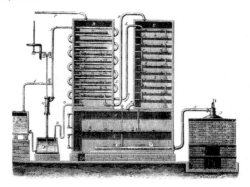

An 1870 illustration showing the workings of a Coffey Still

how Scotch is made

BLENDING

Blending is a slightly separate part of the whisky-making process, with a third product being made from malt and grain whiskies. It both guarantees consistency of the brand and aims to create a new whisky of character in its own right. It is a process which absorbs the greater part of the distilleries' production, and is the mainstay of the industry.

The process was developed on a commercial footing in the second half of the nineteenth century. Although it may initially have been used as a way of stretching further supplies of the more expensive malt whisky, it was the means by which whisky was popularized first in the English market, then overseas.

The blender at work

Blending is an olfactory craft, with blenders nosing rather than tasting whiskies. It is a highly skilled profession, with anything from 20 to 50 different whiskies being mixed in any one brand, including varieties of type, region, distillery and age. The new whisky's character is dependent on how well these different

blending

component whiskies complement and contrast with one another to bring out their various flavours. The high number of component whiskies is the blender's guarantee of consistency: if one contributing distillery goes out of production, the consistency of the blend can be maintained more easily than if there were a

ULTIMA

*A Blend of the Finest
Old Scotch Whiskies*
Distilled Blended & Bottled in Scotland

Justerini & Brooks

By Appointment to Their Late Majesties

70cl ℮   *43% vol.*

The Ultimate Blend of 128 Scotch Whiskies

PRODUCT OF SCOTLAND

*The ultimate blend: J&B Ultima
combines 116 malts and 12 grain
whiskies*

lesser number of whiskies, each with a stronger presence, as ingredients.

The ingredients and their proportions are closely guarded secrets, although it is generally assumed that where a blender owns a distillery, the distillery's produce will be represented to some degree in the blend: so, for example, the produce of Laphroaig Distillery, which is owned by Allied Distillers, is present in their Long John, Ballantine's and Teacher's blends. The produce of some distilleries is never bottled as a single malt, and goes entirely for blending.

After the whiskies are matured, they are mixed together in their correct proportions in a vat, then 'married' in oak casks for at least a year to allow intermingling and further maturation to take place. As with most malts, the blend is reduced to the correct strength by the addition of water. Burnt-sugar caramel may be added to bring a blend up to its desired colour before the whisky is filtered, bottled and labelled.

TYPES OF SCOTCH WHISKY

There are particular legal constraints on what can be termed Scotch whisky, the most basic of which dictate the components of the whisky (cereals, malt and yeast), the maximum alcoholic strength at distillation (94.8% alcohol by volume), and the minimum length of maturation (at least three years). Finally, the whisky itself must have been distilled and matured in Scotland.

Scotland produces two main types of whisky, and all the available varieties of the spirit are variations on these themes. The first is malt whisky, made from malted barley, using a pot still; and the second is grain whisky, made from other cereals – maize or unmalted barley, together with a little malted barley – in a patent still. The two types' distillation processes are explained on pp. 20–30; what follows here is an explanation of the varieties in which they are available.

SINGLE MALTS

A single malt is the product of one distillery. Legally, it can be sold after only three years' maturation, but in practice it is generally left to mature from between eight to fifteen years, by which time its character and flavour has become more pronounced and rounded. Generally, whiskies of varying proof strengths and ages from different casks are mixed together, ensuring a consistent distillery product (as the product of any one distillation will inevitably not be identical to any other), although the age which appears on the

The Macallan and Glenfiddich: two of the most popular single malts

label is always the age of the youngest distillation in the bottle. Malts are diluted from their cask strength (up to mid 60s percentage alcohol by volume) to 40% or 43% for commercial marketing. Single malts comprise a relatively small, although increasing, proportion of the total whisky market.

Single Cask Whiskies

A sub-group of single malt whisky is the single-cask malt. Generally available commercially only through specialist shops and independent merchants (see pp. 53–55), these are whiskies which, as the name suggests, are the produce of one distillation, bottled straight from the cask and not vatted with any other produce from the distillery.

types of Scotch

This process, together with the absence of chill filtration before the whiskies are bottled, ensures that the particular character of a distillery's whisky – and, indeed, of a specific distillation – is unmasked, and greatly emphasized. Supplies of a particular variety or distillation are, by nature, finite. This is the most expensive type of whisky, often costing at least double the price of a normal, distillery-bottled single malt, but felt by many whisky drinkers to be well worth the expense.

A typical Cadenhead's single-cask bottling of a single malt

VATTED MALTS

A vatted malt is the final of the malt whisky sub-groups. This type of whisky has a long pedigree, having formed the basis of the first blended whisky in the mid nineteenth century. Vatted malts are normally produced by blenders and big companies who have a variety of malt distilleries from which to take their product. It could be regarded as a half-way house between a blend and a single malt, although the flavours in some vatted malts can be just as well developed as those in a single. Single malts of different distilleries and different ages are mixed together, the age (if any)

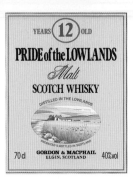

A vatted malt produced by Gordon & MacPhail (top) and The Invergordon, one of the few grain whiskies generally available (below)

on the label being that of the youngest whisky in the mixture. The words 'vatted malt' normally do not appear on a label; instead, the absence of the word 'single' before 'malt', together with an absence of a distillery name, is generally an indicator of a vatted malt.

GRAIN WHISKY

Grain whisky has been mentioned briefly above, and in proportion to the quantities in which it is produced, very little of it is bottled in its own right. Instead, its main function is as a component part of a blend.

BLENDS

Blended whiskies are a mixture of malt and grain, not necessarily in any fixed proportions but rather in a recipe which will achieve the blender's desired balance in terms of character,

types of Scotch

cost and quality. Blends were the means in the nineteenth century by which hitherto too-strongly flavoured malt whiskies were mellowed for the palate in markets outside Scotland – firstly for England, then for export markets. The desired aim of a blender is not to dilute or diminish the flavours of the various component whiskies, but rather to choose ones which are both compatible and complementary, resulting in the creation of a new whisky of distinctive character. In this way, consistency of the product can also be assured. Blended whiskies, of which there are over a thousand, comprise the greater part

Two of the most famous blends anywhere in the world

of the whisky market. The major blenders generally own both malt and grain distilleries, so it is safe to assume that the product of a particular malt distillery will be represented to some degree in its owner's blends.

DE LUXE WHISKIES

A de luxe whisky is a particular type of blend, recognized to be of superior quality to a standard blend. De luxe whiskies generally contain a higher proportion of malt which is older, more mature and consequently more expensive. Some de luxes carry an age statement on their label; as with other whiskies, this is the age of the youngest component in the bottle.

Chivas Regal, a classic de luxe blend

One of the most famous of all liqueur whiskies

LIQUEURS

Blends, but of a quite different type, is a name which can be given to the growing market for whisky liqueurs. Some of these contain whisky flavoured with honey, fruits, herbs and spices, while the cream liqueurs also contain whisky, but are more inclined towards cream, coffee and chocolate in their flavours.

REGIONAL CHARACTERISTICS OF SCOTCH MALT WHISKY

The qualities and characteristics associated with particular producing regions are not a result of current tastes and fashions, but rather a legacy of the past. In times when roads were often poor or, at some times of the year, non-existent, when communications were often difficult, sometimes dangerous and always time-consuming, and trade between different parts of the country was expensive, it was obvious that a distillery would use the raw materials and ingredients which were to hand in a particular locality rather than go to the trouble of importing produce from other areas. These factors, combined with local climate and geology, helped produce whiskies which varied in character from one part of the country to another.

The current chief distinction, between Highland and Lowland whiskies, is also a legacy of a past legal and fiscal policy. As a means of controlling the trade and movement of whisky from the Highlands to the Lowlands (whose cheaper, coarser grain spirit was then successfully being exported into England), the Highland dividing line was established, following roughly the Highland Boundary Fault Line, which runs from the Firth of Clyde to the Firth of Tay. The distinction remained, even with the equalizing of quality between malts from north and south of the line, and it is still recognized today.

The maps on pp. 42–43 and 48–49 show all existing distilleries within the broad categorizations that follow.

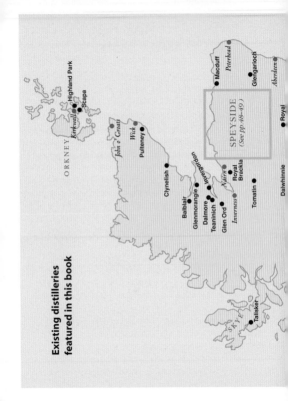

Existing distilleries featured in this book

ORKNEY

Highland Park
Kirkwall
Scapa

Macduff
Peterhead
Glengarioch
Aberdeen

SPEYSIDE
(See pp. 48–49)

John o' Groats

Wick

Pulteney

Clynelish

Nairn
Royal
Brackla

Balblair
Glenmorangie
Invergordon
Dalmore
Teaninich
Glen Ord

Royal

Inverness

Dalwhinnie

Tomatin

SKYE

Talisker

regional characteristics

LOWLAND

Lowland malts are defined as those coming from the southern half of Scotland, that is, south of the Highland line. In terms of their taste, the Lowland malts are perhaps a good first stepping stone for the drinker who wants to graduate from blends: relatively unassertive in character, they are generally soft and light, with a gentle sweetness which ensures them many fans among more experienced palates. Much of the produce of the Lowland malt distilleries is used in blends.

CAMPBELTOWN

Campbeltown was once a major centre of whisky production. Over twenty distilleries operated there in the later nineteenth century, encouraged by the abundance of local supplies of peat, barley from the Mull of Kintyre, and a nearby source of cheap coal. However, over-production, too-wide variations in quality and the exhaustion of the local coal seam contributed to the decline of the local industry, to the point where only two distilleries now remain. With the shift in emphasis from sea-borne to road traffic, it is unlikely that the town will ever again regain its former eminence. Nevertheless, it still retains its regional classification. Campbeltown whiskies are generally accepted to be quite distinctive, with a character which is mellower than that of the Islay malts, with a smoothness and a variable peatiness in the flavour.

ISLAY

Islay malts must be, for everyone from the beginner to the connoisseur, the most distinctive of all single malt whiskies –

certainly, their flavour is among the strongest of all the regions. Peat is the key, both in terms of its influence on the ingredients used for distillation and of its presence in the final taste. The island has extensive beds of peat, over which the water used in the distillation process flows, arriving at its destination already flavoured. Varying amounts of peat are also used to dry the barley. In the past this latter ingredient, too, was produced locally, although now it may be brought in. Peat is noticeable in the flavours of all the Islay malts, from the mildest to the most intensely flavoured, imparting a dryness which is sometimes balanced by sweetness, sometimes emphasized by smokiness. For beginners to single malts, the Islay whiskies seem like an acquired taste, but they are an essential ingredient in the whisky-blending process, and the chances are that what you may think of as the distinctively Scottish flavour in your whisky is imparted by their presence in a blend.

HIGHLAND

Finally, the largest region, with more distilleries than the rest of the country combined, is Highland, probably the quintessential Scottish whisky production area. This is the land which lies to the north of the Highland line and includes distilleries as far apart as Inchmurrin in Dunbartonshire, Oban in Argyll, Pulteney in Wick and Highland Park in Orkney. As might be expected across such a wide area, generalizations become less valid and sub-division becomes more necessary. Geographical divisions of north, south, east and west, together with a special one for Speyside, can be useful in illustrating particular characteristics.

regional characteristics

North, South, East and West Highlands

The north Highland malts can be said to stretch from the area around Inverness up the east coast to Wick. The whiskies from this area are generally smooth, and while ranging from dry to fruity sweet, are not normally quite as peaty as some of their more southerly neighbours. Whisky from the southern Highlands – generally speaking, around the Perthshire area and to the west – is, as might be expected, softer and lighter in character, often reasonably sweet but with one or two dry examples. The western Highlands is the smallest of the Highland sub-divisions, encompassing the area from Oban to Fort William with their smooth, rounded whiskies. The eastern Highlands has distilleries spread out along the North Sea coast from Brechin in the south to Banff in the north. The whiskies in this area offer a wide range of styles, one of the widest of any of the sub-divisions, from fruity sweetness to peaty dryness.

Speyside

The largest and most famous of the Highland sub-divisions is that of Speyside, producing a range of single malts whose names are instantly recognizable, even to non-whisky drinkers: Macallan, Glenfiddich, Glenfarclas and Glenlivet. The area is concentrated around the Elgin–Dufftown district, a picturesque and fertile area whose remoteness made it an ideal location for the whisky smugglers of past centuries to escape the efforts of the excisemen. Speyside whiskies are recognized as being mellow, with a malty sweetness and light notes of peat: beyond this basic generalization, however, lies a wealth of variety and subtlety, and the Speyside

regional characteristics

malts can range from the aromatic and flowery to the robust and sherried. Whiskies can be found in this area to satisfy all palates, from the novice to the connoisseur, and for all occasions.

Island

The final Highland sub-group is that of the Island whiskies. As might be expected when these are viewed on a map, the classification is not so much based on characteristics as convenience – this is a suitable sub-group in which to deal with the remaining whiskies which do not fit in any other.

At present, the islands concerned are Jura, Mull and Skye in the west, and Orkney in the north. (It does not, of course, include Islay, whose distinctive style merits a category of its own.) However, in 1995 the Isle of Arran was added to this list with the opening of the first legal distillery on the island for 160 years at Lochranza. (The single malt produced here was not due to be available early in the 21st century but the distillery's microclimate allowed the whisky to mature at a faster rate than originally expected and the first bottles of Arran Single Malt were launched in 1999.) Once again, generalizations are difficult to make, with characters ranging from reasonably dry to full, sweet and malty.

As with any classification, these listings should not be taken as hard-and-fast rules – taste and preferences vary so greatly that they can only be general guidelines. The best way to decide how well particular whiskies fit their supposed regional listing or characteristic is simply to try each one for yourself!

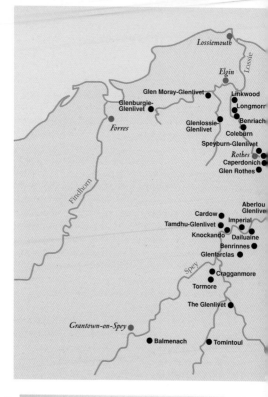

Lossiemouth

Lossie

Elgin

Glen Moray-Glenlivet
Linkwood
Glenburgie-
Glenlivet
Longmorn
Benriach
Glenlossie-
Glenlivet
Coleburn

Forres

Speyburn-Glenlivet
Rothes
Caperdonich
Glen Rothes

Findhorn

Aberlou
Glenlive
Cardow
Imperial
Tamdhu-Glenlivet
Knockando
Dailuaine
Benrinnes
Glenfarclas

Spey
Cragganmore
Tormore

The Glenlivet

Grantown-on-Spey
Balmenach
Tomintoul

48

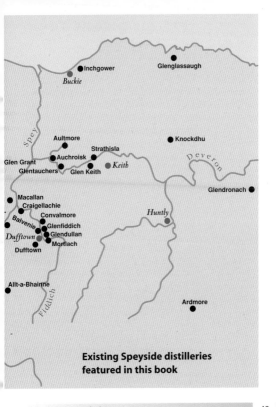

Existing Speyside distilleries featured in this book

VISITING SCOTCH DISTILLERIES AND PRODUCERS

With more than 1,000,000 people visiting Scotland's distilleries every year, catering for visitors has become an important means of promotion and source of revenue for the more famous whisky-makers. Many distilleries are happy to accept visitors, and facilities range from a friendly, impromptu guided tour to a high-tech reception centre with organized tour and gift shop.

Ardbeg Distillery, silent for many years, is now restored and operational, and welcoming visitors

Springbank Distillery, one of several welcoming visitors by appointment only

Once you have decided which distilleries you would like to visit, you can telephone in advance to find out the particular facilities they offer – the telephone numbers of those distilleries which are equipped to receive visitors are given under their entries throughout the book. It is particularly advisable to telephone if you plan to visit during July and August. Although this is the height of the tourist season, it is also the traditional 'silent' period for this industry which was so closely associated with farming: closing the distillery at this time meant that the workers could help to gather in the harvest.

The Scotch Whisky Association website (www.scotch-whisky.org.uk) has full details of over forty distilleries which welcome visitors, together with opening times and booking information. Scotland's national tourism board, VisitScotland (contact centre,

visiting

tel: 0845 22 55 121) is also a useful source of information, as is the Aberdeen & Grampian Tourist Board, whose website (www.maltwhiskytrail.com) provides suggestions for itineraries taking in a selection of Speyside distilleries.

If you are in Edinburgh, a visit to the Scotch Whisky Heritage Centre (tel: 0131-220 0441; www.whisky-heritage.co.uk) on Castlehill is always a good starting point if you want to find out more about the industry, with exhibits and events that are both fun and educational. You can travel back through the industry's past, including the days of illicit distillation, viewing all from the comfort of your own motorized whisky cask!

Finally, for the opportunity to see a perfectly preserved traditional distillery, Dallas Dhu at Forres should not be missed if you are

travelling through the north east. Established at the end of the nineteenth century, it was previously owned by the Distillers Company, who closed it in 1983, and is now operated by Historic Scotland. While it no longer produces whisky, it offers one of the most interesting distillery visits in Scotland (telephone: 01309-676548 for opening times).

Glenmorangie Distillery which boasts first-class visitor facilities

visiting

PROFESSIONAL BODIES, MERCHANTS AND TRADE ASSOCIATIONS

As explained on pp. 35–36, single malts bottled by the distilleries are generally a marrying of casks from several distillations, with water being added to reduce the whisky to an agreed alcohol by volume strength for bottling. The whisky will also generally undergo a process of cold-temperature filtration to remove the residues which naturally precipitate cloudiness in the drink after dilution, when it is kept at low temperatures, or when it has ice added. Views differ as to whether this alters the character and taste of the whisky: the producers cite scientific evidence to show that there is no alteration to the whisky's character if it is not diluted below 40% alcohol by volume. However, various independent bodies believe that it does, and they offer consumers the chance to test for themselves.

THE SCOTCH MALT WHISKY SOCIETY

The Scotch Malt Whisky Society (tel: 0131-554 3451; www.smws.com) is one of these bodies. It buys from the distilleries selected single malts which it bottles straight from the cask and offers to its members, of whom there are over 18,000 around the world. The society aims to promote the increased understanding, appreciation and discerning consumption of malt whisky and has recently begun day-long whisky schools comprising practicals, lectures and tastings.

WILLIAM CADENHEAD

The independent spirit merchants, William Cadenhead Ltd (tel: 01586-554258; www.wmcadenhead.com), also subscribe to this view of the chill-filtration process, and pride themselves on maintaining the individuality of each batch of whisky, bottling straight from the cask at cask strength. The company's approach, of minimal interference with the whisky, relatively simple packaging, and the taking of care over content rather than presentation, is designed to appeal to the slightly more experienced whisky drinker. Much of Cadenhead's stock comes from distilleries whose produce is not otherwise available to the public.

GORDON AND MACPHAIL

Gordon and MacPhail of Elgin (tel: 01343-545111; www.gordonandmacphail.com) also offer a wide range of their own bottlings from many distilleries. The company, owned and run by the Urquhart family, was established in 1895 as a wine and spirit merchant and licensed grocers, and now is regarded as the world's leading malt whisky specialists. Gordon and MacPhail's policy has always been to buy new whisky direct from a distillery, often in their own casks, warehousing it themselves and bottling it when they consider it to be at its best. Each barrel is assessed for quality, style and quantity available prior to bottling, thereby achieving a consistency and quality of malt for which the company is recognized.

professional bodies

SIGNATORY VINTAGE SCOTCH WHISKY COMPANY

A relative newcomer to the independent merchants' ranks is the Signatory Vintage Scotch Whisky Company, based in Edinburgh (tel: 0131-555 4988). Founded in the late 1980s, they acquire casks of exceptional age and quality and bottle either diluted to 40%, 43% or 46%, or at cask strength. No colourant is used in their bottlings and only the diluted range is chill-filtered to remove oiliness. There is a variation between bottlings as the number of casks vatted varies.

THE MINI BOTTLE CLUB

For those whose interest is in the packaging as much as the contents, The Mini Bottle Club is the world's premier club for collectors of miniatures. Membership details can be obtained by emailing minibottleclub@aol.com

SCOTCH WHISKY ASSOCIATION

Finally, if you would like to know more about any aspect of Scotch whisky, the Scotch Whisky Association will happily supply information for you. The association promotes the interests of the Scotch whisky industry in Britain and around the world, and its membership comprises almost all companies involved in the industry. The Public Affairs office is in London (tel: 020 7629 4384), while the head office is in Edinburgh (tel: 0131-222 9200). Its website can be found at www.scotch-whisky.org.uk.

READING THE LABEL

The label on a whisky bottle will allow you to identify a few basic facts about its contents even before you open the bottle – most obviously, the brand and its producers, the type of whisky it is, and its age, quantity and strength. Single malts normally proclaim themselves as such, and the identification of the producing distillery acts as a double check. A label which states a bottle's contents to be malt, but without the words 'single' or 'unblended', is probably vatted. Grains and blends likewise will identify themselves, and while most de luxe whiskies will also do so, this is not always the case. Blends of all kinds will carry the name of the blenders rather than of any distillery.

Where whiskies carry an age statement on the label, this will be the age of the youngest whisky in the bottle. Instead of this, some malts may give the year of their distillation. Single malts are usually eight years old and upwards, becoming more expensive as their age increases. It is generally held, however, that up to fifteen years is a good maturation period for whisky, and while some whiskies improve by maturing beyond this period, not all do of necessity – it depends on the individual whisky. Whiskies for general consumption in the UK are normally packaged in 70 or 75 cl bottles, but you may also come upon 1 litre bottles.

Most whiskies are sold at 40% alcohol by volume. The system for measuring spirit strength in Britain changed in 1980 from the older and more complicated Sikes system of measuring proof

reading the label

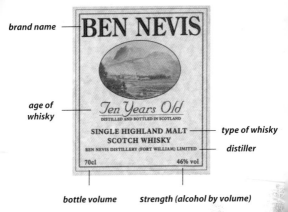

brand name — BEN NEVIS

age of whisky — *Ten Years Old*
DISTILLED AND BOTTLED IN SCOTLAND

SINGLE HIGHLAND MALT
SCOTCH WHISKY — **type of whisky**

BEN NEVIS DISTILLERY (FORT WILLIAM) LIMITED — **distiller**

70cl   46% vol

bottle volume   **strength (alcohol by volume)**

The component parts of a single malt whisky label

strength, to the Organization of Legal Metrology, or OIML system, which measures spirit strength as a percentage of volume at 20°C. Whisky is distilled at a much higher content than its final form for consumption. Water may be added before it goes into the cask, to bring it down to 68.5% alcohol by volume, a standard measure. Some evaporation takes place as the whisky matures, leaving a final cask strength of around 45–60%. Cask-strength whiskies are available, but most single malts have to have water added to bring them down to 40% or 43% (normally for the export market) strength for bottling. However, the industry may move towards a standard strength of 40% after a 1988 European Community directive which based the amount of duty on the alcoholic strength of a spirit. 40% alcohol by volume is equivalent to the old measure of 70° proof and, confusingly, 80° proof in the USA, which uses a slightly different system again.

reading the label

DEVELOPING THE PALATE
by Una Holden-Cosgrove

Apart from the anatomical meaning – the roof of the mouth – a palate refers to the sense of taste, but the roof of the mouth does play an important role in discerning a taste. Spicy, hot and cold, pleasant and objectionable sensations are all in the province of the palate. Everyone has a different reaction to taste and both physically and psychologically the sense of smell has a major influence on how these sensations are perceived.

Where whisky is concerned, a palate needs to be educated in the same way as it must gradually be introduced to the different foods encountered in different countries – after all, a vindaloo is hardly the best introduction to curries! Similarly, a dram of one whisky

can never be regarded as a real experience or a satisfactory introduction to the elixir of life. Every whisky has a different taste and smell: some are quite fierce, or vigorous, and others more honeyed and enticing. To attempt one of the more powerful malts, such as The Glenlivet or Talisker, without any previous knowledge of whisky can only kill any interest in proceeding further.

Unfortunately the early writers on whisky overlooked the fact that their palates were accustomed to the differing tastes and had been conditioned so that the robust types were more to their particular liking. As a result the malts and blends they recommended so highly were usually too powerful for the beginner, leading to an undeservedly macho image for malt whisky which meant that these stronger whiskies were more commonly found on the shelves of bars outside Scotland.

An ideal way to demonstrate this difference in taste is used at whisky-tasting sessions, where the participants are gently guided through a series of malts, starting with the softer, fruity smelling ones and slowly working through to the stronger ones. With this manipulation of the palate, almost invariably the participants find the final dram the most appealing! As these participants do not always appreciate that the aim of tastings is to show how good even the stronger malts are when the palate has been tutored, they are liable to seek out the strongest one to try again at a later date, only to find it tastes too strong – their palate has not really developed sufficiently to cope with it without more experience. So how should a palate be developed?

It is perhaps advisable to start with a whisky mix, as long as the whisky is a blend, or a grain such as Invergordon, and not a malt. Lemonade, soda, even water and ice are possible mixes for blended whisky. This will begin to train the senses and on cold days a Whisky Mac (blended whisky and Green Ginger) will provide a feeling of warmth that goes hand in hand with other pleasant sensations. A really fine blend – such as Black Bottle – can then be attempted neat.

developing the palate

Graduation to a malt requires good company and careful thought. For most beginners the spirit should not assail the taste buds, but inveigle the senses through an appealing scent, subtle taste and soothing after-effects. The aroma, which should be savoured before a sip is taken, can be spicy, fruity, flowery or peaty, and as with other scents like perfume and aftershave, individual preferences must be considered. The taste for the inexperienced should not be fierce – instead, the malt should be chosen from among the smooth, velvety and honeyed selections. Some are dry and others a little sweet, and once again personal preference must be recognized.

After-effects are every bit as important, as the palate can be attacked some time after a stronger malt has been imbibed, and this can be unpleasant to the unwary. There are a variety of exciting after-effects that should be experienced and appreciated. The sparkles on the tongue and roof of the mouth provided by such malts as Oban and Aberlour are quite delightful, the feeling of being massaged, not just in the mouth but all over the shoulders and back, as produced by such as Glendullan after only one sip will help to cure most stress reactions. There are sensations of glowing warmth in the mouth, further reminiscent tastes of fruit or other pleasant foods and even a very delayed sharpness that comes as an unexpected surprise.

developing the palate

The use of miniatures is extremely helpful in identifying whiskies that appeal most to an individual. Further tutoring of the palate should be by experiencing the stronger ones in graduated steps, rather than by assaulting an unprepared and unsuspecting mouth!

Very simply, to drink a malt whisky properly, in order to obtain maximum enjoyment, it is necessary to consider the smell, taste and after-effects that would appeal to a particular individual. Time should be spent appreciating the aroma, taking only a small sip, letting it roll around the mouth before swallowing it and then awaiting the enjoyment of its after-effects. It is also well to remember that mood and the time of day as well as the weather conditions play a role in palate appeal. What may at the end of a horrible day seem like the most wonderful malt on earth, could well appear boring and inadequate on a cold winter's night or overwhelming in the middle of a happy gathering on a glorious summer's afternoon. Remember, too, that a palate will change with experience.

There are many, many blends, a few grain whiskies, a number of vatted malts and about 160 single malts (from approximately 120 distilleries, with some producing more than one year and volume) from which to choose. All are different, each with a different effect on different palates and providing the customer with a wonderful choice and opportunity to learn about a fascinating topic. If the beginner treats whisky with respect, the experiences encountered in the process of development will prove enchanting.

developing the palate

THE WHISKIES
OF SCOTLAND

TASTE RATING

The discussions on the different whiskies which follow contain a taste rating of 1–5. This is not intended to be a judgement on the quality or relative standard of the spirit, nor is it possible to place strength and flavour together satisfactorily. Rather, it can be used as an indicator of accessibility of the whisky for a relatively inexperienced palate. A whisky may be mild or strong and still either lack flavour or exude it, so this rating concerns the degree of flavour, while at the same time allowing for the strength interfering with a person's ability to appreciate the flavour. The basic categories are as follows:

1   Popular with particular palates; spirituous, with a very mild flavour

2   Good for beginners; appealing taste and flavour for most palates at certain times

2–3   Also good for beginners, but a little stronger than 2. One to return to again and again

3   A dram for everyone; not too powerful, with pleasant sensations

3–4   This should also appeal to most tastes, but is slightly stronger, so the palate requires a little more experience

4   Very pleasing; a stronger spirit, ideal for those with more experience

5   Robust; only for the well-developed palate

HIGHLAND
SINGLE MALT
SCOTCH WHISKY

ABERFELDY

distillery was established in 1898 on the road to Perth and north side of the RIVER TAY. Fresh spring water is taken from the nearby PITILIE burn and used to produce this UNIQUE single MALT of SCOTCH WHISKY with its distinctive PEATY nose.

A G E D **15** Y E A R S

Distilled & Bottled in SCOTLAND
ABERFELDY DISTILLERY
Aberfeldy, Perthshire, Scotland
43% vol 70cl

ABERFELDY

Aberfeldy Distillery, Aberfeldy, Perthshire

• AGE •

12, 15 years

• STRENGTH •

40%, 43%

• TASTE RATING •

3

• COMMENTS •

Basically a dry malt with a medium body and clean, fresh character, but with a distinctly peaty background.

• VISITORS •

Visitors are welcome to Dewar's World of Whisky at Aberfeldy Distillery. 1000–1800 Mon.–Sat. 1200–1600 Sun. Times vary in winter. Telephone 01887-822010.

Aberfeldy Distillery stands near the River Tay, at the town from which it takes its name. Building began in 1896 and the distillery opened two years later. It was built by Dewar and passed with that company into the ownership of the Distillers Company Ltd in 1925. Almost all of its production traditionally went into blends. The single malt is available in the Distillery (Flora and Fauna) Malts series and, since Dewar's was sold to drinks group Bacardi by former owners Diageo in 1998, in a new distillery bottling.

ABERLOUR

**Aberlour Distillery,
Aberlour, Banffshire**

• AGE •

10, 12, 16 years and A'bunadh

• STRENGTH •

40%, 43%

• TASTE RATING •

3

• COMMENTS •

A smooth, rich, sherried
Speyside malt which is an
ideal after-dinner drink.

• VISITORS •

Visitors are welcomed
by appointment.
Admission £7.50.
Tours begin at
1030 and 1400 Mon.–Sat.
and 1130 and 1500 on Sun.
Telephone: 01340-871204.

Aberlour was built in the 1860s below Ben Rinnes from whose slopes it draws its water, said to be an important characteristic of its distinctive flavour. In the distillery grounds is the well of tenth-century St Drostan (or Dunstan), missionary and patron saint of Aberlour who later became Archbishop of Canterbury. Since its 1974 acquisition by Pernod, Aberlour has been one of the most popular whiskies in France, the UK and the USA. Aberlour 10 Years Old has recently won the prestigious trophy for 'Best Single Malt Scotch Whisky Under 12 Years Old' at the International Wine & Spirit Competition 2003.

single malt

ALLT-A-BHAINNE

Allt-a-Bhainne Distillery, Glenrinnes, Banffshire

• AGE •

Varies

• STRENGTH •

Varies

• TASTE RATING •

3

• COMMENTS •

A sweet, slightly oaky nose with a touch of vanilla is followed by strong vanilla flavours on the palate. Available only from independent bottlers.

Allt-a-Bhainne is one of the newer Speyside distilleries. Built by Chivas in 1975 to supply malt for its blends, the distillery's produce has never been officially released as a single malt, although independent bottlings are available. The name means *burn of milk* in Gaelic, and the distillery takes its water from the nearby Scurran and Rowantree burns. Allt-a-Bhainne was extended in 1989 but was mothballed in 2002 after Pernod's acquisition of Chivas.

AN CNOC

Knockdhu Distillery, Knock, Banffshire

• AGE •
10, 12 years

• STRENGTH •
40%

• TASTE RATING •
2–3

• COMMENTS •
An Cnoc's dryish aroma is complemented by a mellow sweetness in the flavour. This Highland malt was previously known under its distillery name of Knockdhu.

• VISITORS •
The distillery is not open to visitors.

Knockdhu Distillery was established in 1893 on a favoured site, with water available from Knock Hill, barley from the nearby farmlands, and a good supply of local peat. Although both buildings and machinery have since been modified, the production process remains essentially the same, with the two originally designed pot stills remaining. In 1988 Knockdhu was bought by Inver House Distillers who reopened it after a lengthy silent period.

single malt

THE ANTIQUARY

Tomatin Distillery Company, Tomatin, Inverness-shire

Sanderson, the producers of The Antiquary, was one of the blending companies which started in the early–mid nineteenth century and who were responsible for the popularizing of blended whiskies in the lucrative markets of southern England. William Sanderson was also a founder of the North British Distillery company in 1885 which ensured supplies of good grain whisky for his blends.

de luxe

ARDBEG

**Ardbeg Distillery,
Port Ellen, Islay, Argyllshire**

• AGE •
Varies

• STRENGTH •
Varies

• TASTE RATING •
5

• COMMENTS •
With a dominant peaty aroma and salty, orangey overtones, Ardbeg's insistently smoky flavour is balanced by sweeter notes.

• VISITORS •
Visitors are welcome 1000–1600 Mon.–Fri. all year. Extended hours in summer. Telephone 01496-302418 for details.

The distillery was opened in 1815, one of several established near the sea in an area which was used by smugglers. It was bought by Hiram Walker in the 1950s mainly to use its produce in blending; blenders use Islay malts in the way that a chef might use a strong flavour like garlic. Nearby Lochs Uigeadale and Arinambeast supply the water which, together with local peat, produces a distinctively Islay malt. After Glenmorangie bought Ardbeg from Allied Distillers in 1997 the distillery was restored and an official distillery bottling launched.

single malt

ARDMORE

**Ardmore Distillery,
Kennethmont, Aberdeenshire**

The distillery at Ardmore was built in 1898 by the Teacher family of whisky blenders and merchants. Since that time almost all its production has gone into Teacher's blends, most famously Highland Cream. Today it is operated by Allied Distillers, so its product also features prominently in Allied's other blends. Although the distillery has been modernized, it still retains its traditions and some of the original equipment, such as coal-fired stills, used in the production of whisky at the end of the nineteenth century.

• AGE •
Varies

• STRENGTH •
4

• TASTE RATING •
3

• COMMENTS •
A richly aromatic malt with a floral nose and an underlying grassiness. Not an easy whisky to come by; available as a single malt only through independent bottlers.

• VISITORS •
Visitors are welcome by appointment 1200–1630 Mon.–Sat. May–Sept. Extended hours July & Aug. Telephone 01464-831213 to arrange.

THE ARRAN MALT

Isle of Arran Distillery, Lochranza, Isle of Arran

• AGE •

12 years

• STRENGTH •

40%

• TASTE RATING •

2

• COMMENTS •

A malt of characteristic Arran sweetness from its faintly tart, appley nose through into its slightly toffee flavours. A pre-dinner dram.

• VISITORS •

Visitors are welcome at the award-winning visitor centre. Tours are held daily. 1000–1800, mid-Mar.–end Oct. Reduced opening hours in Nov. and Dec. Telephone 01770-830264 for details.

This new malt from the Isle of Arran Distillers has been acclaimed by whisky writers around the world. Isle of Arran Distillers are a dynamic and independent new player in the Scotch whisky industry. Their distillery on Arran at Lochranza opened in 1995 and the company now successfully markets its portfolio of blends and malts throughout Europe, Asia and the American continent. In common with only a few other distillers, Isle of Arran also produce a non-chill filtered variant of their malt.

AUCHENTOSHAN

Auchentoshan Distillery, Dalmuir, Dunbartonshire

• AGE •

10, 12 years and others

• STRENGTH •

40%, 43%

• TASTE RATING •

2–3

• COMMENTS •

A light, sweetish whisky whose smooth qualities are perhaps partially owed to the process of triple, rather than the more common double distillation.

• VISITORS •

The distillery is not open to visitors.

Although Auchentoshan lies south of the Highland Line (the line initiated by the Customs and Excise to differentiate area boundaries between styles of whisky), it uses water from north of the line, and so could be said to have a foot in both camps. It is, however, officially recognized as a Lowland distillery and whisky. Founded in the early nineteenth century, its severest challenge came when it was bombed during the Clydebank Blitz in the Second World War, and a stream of blazing whisky was said to have flowed from the building. It is presently owned by Morrison Bowmore.

AUCHROISK

**Auchroisk Distillery,
Mulben, Banffshire**

SPEYSIDE
SINGLE MALT
SCOTCH WHISKY

*In a striking hilltop location, visible from
ROTHES, is sited the*

AUCHROISK

*distillery. The unusual name, meaning 'FORD of
the RED STREAM' in Gaelic, refers to the
MULBEN BURN from which the distillery draws
its cooling water. However, the principal reason
for the siting of the distillery is DORIE'S WELL,
an abundant source of soft, pure springwater.
Through the smoke and nutty sweetness, comes the
unmistakeable feel of DORIE'S silky water,
followed by a dry, well balanced finish.*

AGED **10** YEARS

43% vol   70 cl

• **AGE** •

10 years

• **STRENGTH** •

43%

• **TASTE RATING** •

2–3

• **COMMENTS** •

*This whisky is medium-bodied,
with fresh, nutty hints to its
flavour, which is smooth and
sweet, and balanced by
a short finish.*

• **VISITORS** •

*Visitors are welcome
1000–1600 Mon.–Fri.
by appointment only.
Telephone 01542-860333
to arrange.*

One of the newest Scottish distilleries (opened in 1974), Auchroisk was built by what was then International Distillers and Vintners. The building has won several awards, including one from the Angling Foundation for not interfering with the upriver progress of salmon. Dorie's Well provides the distillery with its pure, natural water source. From 1987 the company marketed its award-winning single under the name of The Singleton of Auchroisk, but it has recently been rebranded as part of Diageo's Distillery (Flora and Fauna) Malts series.

     single malt

SPEYSIDE
SINGLE MALT *SCOTCH* WHISKY

AULTMORE

distillery located between KEITH and BUCKIE began production in 1897. The name, derived from the Gaelic, means "big burn". Ideal supplies of water and peat from the Foggy Moss made this area a haunt of illicit distillers in the past. Water from the Burn of AUCHINDERRAN is now used to produce this smooth, well balanced single MALT ⅓2 SCOTCH WHISKY with a mellow finish.

AGED 12 YEARS

43% vol *Distilled & Bottled in SCOTLAND. AULTMORE DISTILLERY. Keith, Banffshire, Scotland.* 70 cl

AULTMORE

**Aultmore Distillery,
Aultmore, Keith, Banffshire**

• AGE •

12 years

• STRENGTH •

43%

• TASTE RATING •

3

• COMMENTS •

A faintly peaty aroma leads into a smooth, fruity, well-balanced whisky.

• VISITORS •

The distillery is open to visitors by appointment only. Telephone 01542-881800 to arrange.

Aultmore Distillery was established in 1895 at the tail-end of the whisky boom by the owner of the older Benrinnes Distillery. The area, with its abundant peat and water supplies, was infamous in the past for illicit distilling. Peat used in the production process is taken from a nearby moss, and the water from local springs. The distillery passed to Dewars in 1923, and was improved and upgraded in the 1970s. It was sold to drinks group Bacardi by Diageo in 1998, but the single malt is still available in Diageo's Distillery (Flora and Fauna) Malts series.

THE BAILIE NICOL JARVIE

Macdonald and Muir, Leith, Edinburgh

• AGE •
6 years

• STRENGTH •
40%

• TASTE RATING •
2

• COMMENTS •
A light, subtle whisky with a sweet, well-balanced aroma and a smooth, lingering finish.

Founded in 1893, Macdonald and Muir Ltd is one of the few remaining independent, family-owned and controlled companies left in the Scotch whisky business. The Bailie, or BNJ as it is also known, is named after the fictional magistrate in Walter Scott's *Rob Roy*. A popular brand during the Boer War at the turn of the twentieth century, its production was limited until as late as 2002 but is now much more widely available than before. Its high malt content and its use of top-quality malts combine to give a smooth, complex blend.

blend

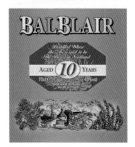

BALBLAIR

**Balblair Distillery,
Edderton, Tain, Ross-shire**

• AGE •

10 years and others

• STRENGTH •

40%

• TASTE RATING •

3

• COMMENTS •

*A distinctive Highland malt
whose slightly dry sharpness
is nicely balanced by a
light note of sweetness.
Good as an aperitif.*

• VISITORS •

*The distillery is not open
to visitors.*

Although its origins are lost in the mists of illicit distillation, it is claimed that Balblair was founded in 1749, which would make it one of the oldest distilleries in the country. The present buildings, dating from the 1870s, are set in pretty countryside in an area known as the 'parish of peats'. The distillery was mothballed by its previous owners, Allied Distillers, but was acquired in 1996 by Inver House, who now own five malt distilleries, all of them working. In 2003 Balblair 33 Year Old won *Whisky* magazine's 'Best of the Best' Scotch whisky accolade.

BALLANTINE'S FINEST

Allied Distillers, Dumbarton, Dunbartonshire

• STRENGTH •
40%, 43%

• TASTE RATING •
2–3

• COMMENTS •

Ballantine's Finest is, like the company's other blends, characteristically mellow and well-rounded with a fruity and sweet flavour. Their range of blends also includes Ballantine's Gold Seal 12-year-old, Ballantine's 17 Years Old and Ballantine's 30-year-old, considered to be the oldest (and most expensive) blend available.

• VISITORS •

The distillery is only open to trade visitors.

Ballantine's was bought in 1936 by Hiram Walker as one of their first moves into the Scotch whisky market. Glenburgie and Miltonduff distilleries followed in 1937 and their new, giant complex in Dumbarton which featured grain and malt distilleries, was operational the following year. Today the group is owned by Allied Domecq and operated by their wholly Scottish-based subsidiary, Allied Distillers. The Dumbarton plant is renowned locally for its 'Scotchwatch' alarm system, comprising 100-odd noisy Chinese geese!

CONNOISSEURS CHOICE

SPEYSIDE
Single Malt Scotch Whisky

DISTILLED AT
BALMENACH
DISTILLERY
Proprietors: John Crabbie & Co. Ltd.

DISTILLED
1987

Specially selected, produced
and bottled by

70cl   Gordon & MacPhail   40% vol
Elgin, Scotland
Product of Scotland

BALMENACH

**Balmenach Distillery,
Cromdale, Moray**

AGE

12 years

STRENGTH

43%

TASTE RATING

4

COMMENTS

*A complicated, full-bodied
malt best suited as an after-
dinner dram. New owners
Inver House may produce
new bottlings.*

VISITORS

*The distillery is not open
to visitors.*

The Balmenach Distillery, in the Haughs of Cromdale, is set in an area long notorious for illicit distilling before the Licensing Act of 1823. Built in 1824 by James McGregor (great-grandfather of Sir Robert Bruce Lockhart, author of the classic 1951 book, *Scotch*), Balmenach was one of the first Highland distilleries to be licensed under the 1823 act. The distillery was sold in 1997 by United Distillers to Inver House; they have restarted operations but not yet produced a single. Bottlings are available in Diageo's Distillery (Flora and Fauna) Malts series.

THE BALVENIE

**Balvenie Distillery,
Dufftown, Keith, Banffshire**

• AGE •

*10 years (Founder's Reserve),
12 years (Doublewood),
15 years (Single Barrel)
21 years (Port Wood)*

• STRENGTH •

Varies

• TASTE RATING •

3–4

• COMMENTS •

*Founder's Reserve has a rich
colour, bouquet and flavour
with a smooth, clean, dry
finish. Doublewood is full-
bodied, yet smooth and
mellow, and Single Barrel,
a harder-to-obtain 15-year-old,
is a single-cask bottling.*

• VISITORS •

*The distillery is sometimes
open to visitors.
To book in advance,
telephone 01340-820373.*

Built in 1892 near the ruins of
fourteenth-century Balvenie Castle
by the Grants of Glenfiddich,
Balvenie Distillery has now been
owned by an independent family
company for five generations.
Balvenie Distillery still grows its own
barley, malts in its own traditional
floor maltings, employs coopers to
tend the barrels and coppersmiths
to tend the stills. The Balvenie produces a range of three malt whiskies
of different age and character.

BANFF

**Banff Distillery,
Banff, Banffshire**

• AGE •

Varies

• STRENGTH •

40%

• TASTE RATING •

2–3

• COMMENTS •

*A light, golden malt with
a fruity nose, spicy palate
and sweet finish.
Available from independent
merchants only.*

This distillery had a colourful history after its founding in 1863. It survived a fire in the 1870s, and bombing during the Second World War, when thousands of gallons of whisky had to be thrown away to stop the spread of fire. It was reported that the whisky ran over the land and into nearby streams, causing drunkenness among the local farm animals and birds, and leaving dairy cows unable to stand for milking! The distillery also once supplied whisky to Parliament. It was closed by the Distillers Company Ltd in 1983 and has been demolished.

single malt

BELL'S EXTRA SPECIAL

**Diageo,
Glasgow**

- AGE -

8 years

- STRENGTH -

40%

- TASTE RATING -

2–3

- COMMENTS -

*The most popular blend in
the UK, Bell's Extra Special is
a pleasant, medium-bodied
whisky with a nutty aroma
and a spicy flavour.*

The merchants and blending company which ultimately became Arthur Bell & Sons started in Perth in 1825, with Bell himself joining the firm as a traveller in the 1840s. By 1851 he was a partner and in 1895 the 'Extra Special' name, with Bell's signature, was registered as a trade mark. Large-scale expansion came in the 1930s when Bell acquired three of the company's subsequent complement of five distilleries. Bell's is now owned by Diageo who, as United Distillers, successfully relaunched Bell's Extra Special as an 8-year-old blend in 1994.

BEN NEVIS

Ten Years Old

DISTILLED AND BOTTLED IN SCOTLAND

SINGLE HIGHLAND MALT
SCOTCH WHISKY

BEN NEVIS DISTILLERY (FORT WILLIAM) LIMITED

70cl   46% vol

BEN NEVIS

**Ben Nevis Distillery,
Fort William, Inverness-shire**

• AGE •

10, 19, 25, 26 years

• STRENGTH •

46%, 56.4%

• TASTE RATING •

3

• COMMENTS •

*Ranging from pale amber to a
deep, golden colour, Ben Nevis
is characterized by its fresh,
slightly peaty flavour and
smooth finish. Ben Nevis's
single malt also features in
the company's blend range,
Dew of Ben Nevis.*

• VISITORS •

*Visitors are welcome
0900–1700 Mon.–Fri. all year
(extended in summer).
Larger parties should
telephone 01397-702476 to
arrange or for more details.*

Ben Nevis is one of the oldest distilleries in Scotland and was founded at Fort William by the famous 'Long' John Macdonald in 1825. After more than 100 years and three generations in the family, the distillery was sold in 1941. The subsequent addition of a patent still made the distillery one of the few that could produce both malt and grain under one roof, and it received a new lease of life in the 1980s following its acquisition by the Nikka Whisky Distilling Co. of Japan.

single malt

BENRIACH

**Benriach Distillery,
Elgin, Moray**

• AGE •

Varies

• STRENGTH •

40%

• TASTE RATING •

4

• COMMENTS •

*A balanced fruity and
spicy malt, with raisins
and chocolate on the palate.
Toasty finish.*

BENRIACH DISTILLERY
EST.1898
A SINGLE
PURE HIGHLAND MALT
Scotch Whisky
Benriach Distillery, in the heart of the Highlands,
still malts its own barley. The resulting whisky has
a unique and attractive delicacy
PRODUCED AND BOTTLED BY THE
BENRIACH
DISTILLERY Cº
ELGIN, MORAYSHIRE, SCOTLAND, IV30 3SJ
Distilled and Bottled in Scotland
AGED 10 YEARS
70 cl ℮ 43% vol

Originally built in the 1890s, Benriach
was closed in 1900 after recession hit
the previously booming whisky
industry. It was refitted and reopened
in 1965, although not completely
modernized, still retaining its hand-
turned malting floor. In fact, until
its recent closure, Benriach was one
of the few distilleries in Scotland
still malting barley on the premises
in the traditional manner. Benriach is
now owned by Chivas Brothers, the
Scotch whisky business of Pernod
Ricard.

BENRINNES

**Benrinnes Distillery,
Aberlour, Banffshire**

• AGE •

15 years

• STRENGTH •

43%

• TASTE RATING •

4

• COMMENTS •

*This is a complex Speyside
malt which has hints of
wood and grass to its flavour,
and a fruity aftertaste.*

• VISITORS •

*The distillery is open to visitors
by appointment only.
Telephone 01340-871215.*

Built almost 700 feet up the slopes
of Ben Rinnes from which it takes
its name, this distillery is believed
to have been founded in 1835
although evidence exists of distilling on this site in 1826. It was largely
rebuilt and modernized in the 1950s.
Most of its production is distilled
three times rather than the more
usual twice, and almost all is used
in Diageo blends. The single malt is
available only in the Distillery (Flora
and Fauna) Malts series.

BENROMACH

**Benromach Distillery,
Forres, Moray**

● AGE ●

18 years

● STRENGTH ●

40%

● TASTE RATING ●

2–3

● COMMENTS ●

*This Speyside malt has a fruity
nose, bringing to mind peaches
and nectarines with a hint of
chocolate malt.*

● VISITORS ●

*Visitors are welcome
1000–1600 Mon.–Fri. all year;
hours extended in summer.
Telephone 01309-675968
for details or visit the
distillery's website:
www.benromach.com*

Benromach was built just outside
Forres in 1898, in the years of expansion for the whisky industry, and it
underwent extensive reconstruction
in 1966 and 1974. It passed through
several hands before coming to rest
with the Distillers Company in 1953.
After ten years in mothballs Benromach
was sold in 1993 to independent
merchants and bottlers Gordon and
MacPhail. Since then it has been refitted, and a new distillation begun in
1996.

single malt

BIG "T"

**Tomatin Distillery Company,
Tomatin, Inverness-shire**

5 years min (standard blend),
12 years de luxe

40%, 43%

1–2 (standard blend),
2–3 (de luxe)

Big "T" standard blend is a
whisky of light-to-medium body
with a fresh, malty sweetness,
well-balanced by a hint
of peat. The 12-year-old de luxe
is an extremely smooth blend,
most of which is reserved
for export.

Visitors are welcome to the
malt whisky distillery; see the
entry on Tomatin for details.

The Tomatin Distillery Company's
premises is not only one of the
highest in the country (standing 1000'
up in the Monadhliath Mountains),
it is also the largest-capacity distillery, with production as high as five
million gallons per annum. The
company declined in the 1980s and
went into receivership, but was
bought by the Japanese firms of
Takara Schuzo and Okura, thus
becoming the first Scotch whisky distillery to be acquired by Japanese
owners. Tomatin have also released
The Talisman, a new, 5 Year Old blend.

BLACK & WHITE

**Diageo,
Banbeath, Leven, Fife**

• STRENGTH •
40%

• TASTE RATING •
2

• COMMENTS •

A clean, pleasantly mild whisky, Black & White has a fresh, grassy flavour which is complemented by a light sweetness.

PRODUCT OF SCOTLAND

Black&White
Choice Old Scotch Whisky

BLENDED, BLENDED AND BOTTLED IN SCOTLAND BY

James Buchanan & Co

GLASGOW & LONDON

43% vol   1 LITRE

Black & White – currently only available outside the UK – is the main blend of what was once James Buchanan's company of London whisky blenders and merchants. It was an instant success, with a contract to supply the House of Commons, and the firm was a leader in introducing blended whiskies to the English market. The distinctive black and white livery earned the whisky's nickname which later became the brand name. The company joined the Distillers Company in 1925, and today its owners are Diageo.

blend

BLACK BOTTLE

Burn Stewart Distillers, Glasgow

• STRENGTH •

40%

• TASTE RATING •

2–3

• COMMENTS •

Black Bottle is a smooth, superior-quality blend with a fresh hint of peat, complemented by sweeter, malty notes.

• VISITORS •

The plant is not suitable for visitors.

Black Bottle was first produced by a family of merchants from Aberdeen in 1879, and has been a premium blend since its first appearance. The company was sold to Long John in 1959, and was acquired by Allied Distillers in 1990 then by Matthew Gloag, producers of The Famous Grouse, before passing into the control of Burn Stewart in 2003. The distinctive pot-still-shaped bottle rapidly became its trademark, and has remained virtually unchanged to the present day.

BLADNOCH

**Bladnoch Distillery,
Bladnoch, Wigtown,
Wigtownshire**

• AGE •

10 years (Flora & Fauna)
23 years (Rare Malt)
15 years (distillery cask
strength Glimpses of
Galloway series)

• STRENGTH •

43%

• TASTE RATING •

2–3

• COMMENTS •

Bladnoch is a light-to-
medium-bodied malt with a
light, fragrant, lemony aroma
and a gentle, unassertive
flavour with fruity tones.

• VISITORS •

Visitors are very welcome
at Bladnoch;
telephone 01988-402605
or visit its website at:
www.bladnoch.co.uk

Scotland's most southerly distillery, Bladnoch, built in 1817, is also one of its oldest. The latest of many owners in the last century is Irishman Raymond Armstrong, who bought it as a holiday home after its closure by United Distillers (now Diageo) in 1993. He began distilling on a limited basis in 2002 and though its single malt will remain rare, bottlings are still available in Diageo's Distillery (Flora and Fauna) Malts series.

single malt

HIGHLAND
SINGLE MALT
SCOTCH WHISKY

BLAIR ATHOL

distillery, established in 1798, stands
on peaty moorland in the foothills of the
GRAMPIAN MOUNTAINS. An ancient
source of water for the distillery, ALLT
DOUR BURN~'The Burn of the Otter',
flows close by. This single MALT
SCOTCH WHISKY has a mellow deep
toned aroma, a strong fruity
flavour and a smooth finish.

Ａｇｅ 12 ｙｅａｒｓ

43% vol   70 cl

BLAIR ATHOL

Blair Athol Distillery,
Pitlochry, Perthshire

• AGE •

12 years

• STRENGTH •

43%

• TASTE RATING •

2–3

• COMMENTS •

*Blair Athol is a light, fresh
single malt with dry notes
and a hint of smokiness.*

• VISITORS •

*Visitors are welcome
1000–1600 Mon.–Sat. all year.
Hours extended to include
weekends in summer, and
restricted in winter.
Telephone 01796-482003
for details or to arrange.*

This is a picturesquely sited distillery on a wooded hillside on the outskirts of the tourist centre of Pitlochry. Blair Athol is unusual in that it is twelve miles distant from the village after which it is named. Established in 1825, the distillery was bought by Bells in 1933 and sympathetically upgraded. It is now owned by Diageo who bottle its malt in their Distillery (Flora and Fauna) Malts series. Its water comes from the Allt Dour (Burn of the Otter) which flows past the distillery en route to the River Tummel.

BOWMORE

**Bowmore Distillery,
Bowmore, Islay, Argyllshire**

• AGE •

*Legend, 12, 15, 17,
25, 40 years and others*

• STRENGTH •

40%, 43%

• TASTE RATING •

3

• COMMENTS •

*With its pleasant aroma
and peaty–fruity flavour,
Bowmore is a good Islay malt
for newcomers to these
distinctive whiskies to try.*

• VISITORS •

*Visitors are welcome by
appointment and tours are
available 1030 and 1400
Mon.–Fri., 1030 Sat. in summer;
1100 and 1530 Mon.–Fri.
the rest of the year.
Telephone 01496-810441
to arrange, or for further details.*

Established in the 1770s, Bowmore is reputed to be the oldest legal distillery on Islay. It stands in the island's main town and overlooks Loch Indaal, and its water is taken from the peaty River Laggan. The distillery passed through several hands in the twentieth century, but has been a thriving concern since its acquisition in 1963 by Stanley P. Morrison of Glasgow. The company is now Morrison Bowmore, and this is their flagship distillery.

BRORA

**Brora Distillery,
Brora, Sutherland**

• AGE •
Varies

• STRENGTH •
40%

• TASTE RATING •
3

• COMMENTS •
A smooth, peaty malt with a smoky palate, finishing slightly sweet and peaty.

Until 1969 Brora was known as Clynelish, when a new distillery built next door assumed the name. The old Victorian distillery was then named Brora and reopened in April 1969. Unfortunately the distillery closed indefinitely in the 1980s, making the exceptional, Islay-style malt produced during its short history extremely rare.

BRUICHLADDICH

**Bruichladdich Distillery,
Bruichladdich, Islay,
Argyllshire**

*10, 15, 17, 20 years
Vintages: various
Full strength*

46% or natural cask strength

3

*Fresh, fruity and fragrant,
Bruichladdich is not chill-filtered,
is bottled using Islay spring
water and is caramel-free.
It is elegant and does not have
the medicinal taste often
associated with Islay malts.*

*Visitors are welcome.
Telephone 01496-850221;
email lorna@bruichladdich.com
or visit the distillery's website:
www.bruichladdich.com*

Bruichladdich (pronounced *brook-laddie*, Gaelic for *raised beach*) dates from 1881 and is Scotland's most westerly distillery. It had a succession of corporate owners until it was deemed 'surplus to requirements' and closed down in 1995. The directors of independent bottlers Murray McDavid, assembled a group of private investors to buy it in December 2000. Bruichladdich produces its lightly peated whisky in the traditional way, using much of the original equipment and is the only Islay-bottled malt.

single malt

BUNNAHABHAIN

**Bunnahabhain Distillery,
Port Askaig, Islay, Argyllshire**

Westering Home

Bunnahabhain
SINGLE ISLAY MALT SCOTCH WHISKY

PRODUCT OF SCOTLAND
THE BUNNAHABHAIN DISTILLERY COMPANY
BUNNAHABHAIN, ISLE OF ISLAY, SCOTLAND. BOTTLED IN SCOTLAND

40% vol.   70 cl

• AGE •

12 years

• STRENGTH •

40%, 43%

• TASTE RATING •

3

• COMMENTS •

*Less characteristically peaty
than some other Islay malts,
Bunnahabhain is a mellow
whisky with hints of spice
and an aromatic flavour.*

• VISITORS •

Visitors are welcome
by appointment
1000–1600 Mon.– Fri.
Telephone 01496-840606
to arrange.

Bunnahabhain, which means 'mouth of the river' in reference to its location on the River Margadale, was founded in 1881 by the Greenlees brothers. They formed the Islay Distillery Company and bought Glenrothes Distillery in 1887, which together formed the Highland Distilleries Company; they in turn sold Bunnahabhain in 2002 to Burn Stewart. The distillery's site was an uninhabited, inhospitable part of the island but over the years a small community has grown up around it.

CAMERON BRIG

Cameronbridge Distillery, Cameron Bridge, Fife

• AGE •

c. 5 years

• STRENGTH •

40%

• TASTE RATING •

1

• COMMENTS •

Like other grain whiskies, a lighter spirit than malt, with a fresh taste and an element of smoothness.

• VISITORS •

The distillery is not suitable for visitors.

Cameronbridge Distillery had been operating for several years before it was acquired in 1824 by John Haig, one of the famous family of Lowland whisky distillers. Haig's company was among the founders of the Distillers Company in 1877; today, Diageo own the distillery. Cameronbridge produced both grain and malt whisky using a mixture of pot and patent stills until 1929 before finally concentrating on grain alone.

ISLAY
SINGLE MALT SCOTCH WHISKY

CAOL ILA

distillery, built in 1846 is situated near Port Askaig on the Isle of Islay.
Steamers used to call twice a week to collect whisky from this remote
site in a cove facing the Isle of Jura. Water supplies for mashing
come from Loch nam Ban although the sea provides water for
condensing. Unusual for an Islay this single MALT SCOTCH
WHISKY has a fresh aroma and a light yet well rounded flavour

AGED 15 YEARS

43% vol Distilled & Bottled in SCOTLAND CAOL ILA DISTILLERY Port Askaig, Isle of Islay, Scotland 70 cl

CAOL ILA

**Caol Ila Distillery,
Port Askaig, Islay, Argyllshire**

• AGE •
15 years

• STRENGTH •
43%

• TASTE RATING •
4

• COMMENTS •
*Nicely balanced, Caol Ila is
not the peatiest of the Islay
whiskies, but is pleasantly dry
with a well-rounded body.*

• VISITORS •
*Visitors are welcome
Mon.–Fri. by appointment.
Telephone 01496-302760
to arrange.*

Caol Ila was established in 1846 and overlooks the Sound of Islay (which is also the English translation of its name). It previously used its own wharf for the despatching of its product. The distillery has been rebuilt twice, at almost 100-year intervals, in 1879 and 1972. The most recent modernization almost doubled the distillery's output. Caol Ila is now owned by Diageo and the single malt has been available in official bottlings since the early 1990s in the Distillery (Flora and Fauna) Malts series.

single malt

CAPERDONICH

**Caperdonich Distillery,
Rothes, Moray**

• AGE •

Varies

• STRENGTH •

Varies

• TASTE RATING •

3–4

• COMMENTS •

*A heavy-fruit aroma lightens
to a mouth-filling flavour
of sweet grapes with
sherried notes with an
afterthought of sweet oak
and cinnamon flavours.*

Originally owned by J & J Grant, this
distillery was built across the road
from their main centre, Glen Grant.
The two distilleries were to be treated
as one for licensing purposes, so a
pipe spanned the road to carry the
produce of Caperdonich (then Glen
Grant No. Two) across for blending.
Built in the boom years of the 1890s,
it suffered the fall-off in consumption in the early 1900s, waiting over
sixty years for renovation, reopening
and its new name of Caperdonich.
It was mothballed in 2003 by new
owners Pernod.

single malt

CARDHU

Cardow Distillery, Knockando, Moray

• AGE •

12 years

• STRENGTH •

40%

• TASTE RATING •

2–3

• COMMENTS •

A smooth, light malt of silky character and delicate, sweet flavour which make it accessible to all from the novice to the connoisseur.

• VISITORS •

Visitors are welcome 0930–1630 Mon.–Fri. all year, and 0930–1630 Sat., 1100–1600 Sun., June–Sept. Shorter hours in winter. Telephone 01340-872555.

Whisky distilling had been carried on illegally in this area for a long time before Cardow Distillery was founded and licensed in 1824. It was bought by John Walker of Kilmarnock during the 1890s boom years, producing a vatted and a single malt under the Gaelicized Cardhu name. The distillery was modernized in 1965 and its single malt was relaunched. It is now owned by Diageo who recently changed the whisky from a single to a vatted malt to meet with overwhelming overseas demand.

vatted malt

CHIVAS REGAL

**Chivas Brothers,
Paisley, Renfrewshire**

• AGE •
12 years

• STRENGTH •
40%

• TASTE RATING •
2–3

• COMMENTS •
*A premium luxury whisky –
a golden amber colour –
smooth, rich and fruity
with delicate floral flavours
and a soft dry nuttiness.*

• VISITORS •
*Visitors are welcome
1000–1600 Mon.–Sat.,
Sun. 1230–1600
Apr.–Oct. inclusive.
Telephone 01542-783044.*

Chivas Regal is the flagship brand of the international Scotch whisky portfolio of Chivas Brothers, Pernod Ricard's Scotch whisky business. The distinctive Chivas Regal style goes all the way back to the nineteenth century, to the Company's founders, James and John Chivas who started business as grocers in the busy trading port of Aberdeen and where they matured and blended their quality whisky in the cellars at the shop. Today, Chivas Regal is sold in over 150 countries.

blend

THE CLAYMORE

Whyte & Mackay Ltd, Glasgow

• STRENGTH •
40%

• TASTE RATING •
2–3

• COMMENTS •

A well-balanced blend with rich highlights both in the nose and on the palate. Rounded off with a fresh finish.

The Claymore is a popular blend which is owned by Whyte & Mackay Ltd, the blending and bottling company begun in 1882 by whisky merchants James Whyte and Charles Mackay. The company was the subject of a management buy-out in 2001. As with many of the company's whiskies, The Claymore is popular in export markets as well as in the UK, where it is among the best-selling blends.

blend

CLYNELISH

**Clynelish Distillery,
Brora, Sutherland**

• AGE •

14 years

• STRENGTH •

43%

• TASTE RATING •

3

• COMMENTS •

A medium-bodied, full-flavoured whisky with many devotees. It is slightly dry to the taste, with a hint of peat. Part of the Distillery (Flora and Fauna) Malts series.

• VISITORS •

Visitors are welcome 0930–1700 Mon.–Fri. (last tour 1600). Hours are restricted in winter and appointments are advised. Telephone 01408-623000.

HIGHLAND
SINGLE MALT
SCOTCH WHISKY

CLYNELISH

distillery, was established in Brora by the Marquess of STAFFORD in 1819. Its building signalled the end of illicit distilling in the area and provided a ready market for locally grown barley. Water is piped from the CLYNEMILTON burn to produce this fruity, & slightly smoky single MALT SCOTCH WHISKY much appreciated by connoisseurs

YEARS 14 O.L.D

43% vol   70cl

The original distillery on this site was built in 1819 by the man who became the 1st Duke of Sutherland, prime mover in the most infamous of the Highland Clearances. Its purpose was to make use of the cheap grain grown on the farms of his recently cleared tenants. A new distillery was built adjacent in 1968, taking the name Clynelish, while the original distillery, renamed Brora, was closed by the Distillers Company Ltd, its parent company, in 1983. It is now owned by Diageo.

single malt

COLUMBA CREAM

The Scottish Liqueur Centre, Bankfoot, Perthshire

Independent, family-owned company John Murray have been producing Columba Cream for several years to a formula which is based on a traditional recipe. As well as Columba Cream, the company produces Murray's Scottish Highland Liqueur and a range of other fruit and whisky liqueurs, all made with pure ingredients and without any concentrates, flavourings, additives or GM ingredients.

• AGE •

5 years

• STRENGTH •

17%

• TASTE RATING •

2

• COMMENTS •

A blend of five single malt whiskies, with the addition of honey and cream makes for a very pleasant and mellow whisky cream liqueur.

• VISITORS •

The visitor centre welcomes visitors; telephone 01738-787044 for details.

liqueur

CONVALMORE

**Convalmore Distillery,
Dufftown, Keith, Banffshire**

• AGE •

Varies

• STRENGTH •

40%

• TASTE RATING •

3

• COMMENTS •

*A medium-bodied spicy,
woody malt with a fruity and
peppery finish. Available from
independent bottlers.*

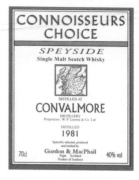

CONNOISSEURS
CHOICE

SPEYSIDE
Single Malt Scotch Whisky

DISTILLED AT

CONVALMORE
DISTILLERY
Proprietors: W P Lowrie & Co Ltd

DISTILLED
1981

Specially selected, produced
and bottled by

Gordon & MacPhail
Elgin   Scotland
Product of Scotland

70cl   40% vol

W. P. Lowrie bought Convalmore in
1904, eleven years after its founding.
After a fire it was rebuilt in 1910 when
experiments were made in the production of malt whisky from patent
stills; this was abandoned in 1916,
however, in favour of the traditional
pot-still method, considered to
mature the whisky better. Almost all
the production of Convalmore goes
into blends. The distillery was acquired
by United Distillers (now Diageo) and
was mothballed in 1985. It is now
owned by William Grant.

CRAGGANMORE

Cragganmore Distillery, Ballindalloch, Banffshire

Cragganmore was built in 1869 and was the first distillery to be built alongside an existing railway and so use the then-new mode of transport for its distribution. The distillery, which took its name from nearby Craggan More Hill, was built by John Smith, a man of such great bulk that he was known locally as 'Cragganmore'. It is now licensed to D & J McCallum. Most of its production goes into blends, especially Old Parr. The distillery now belongs to Diageo.

• AGE •

12 years

• STRENGTH •

40%

• TASTE RATING •

3–4

• COMMENTS •

A Speyside malt of distinctive and complex character, Cragganmore has a delicate aroma and smoky finish.

• VISITORS •

Tours by appointment 1000, 1230 and 1400 Mon.–Fri., June–Sept. Telephone 01479-874700.

CRAIGELLACHIE

**Craigellachie Distillery,
Craigellachie, Aberlour,
Banffshire**

SPEYSIDE
SINGLE MALT
SCOTCH WHISKY

CRAIGELLACHIE

distillery, founded in 1898, in the county of BANFFSHIRE, stands overlooking the RIVER SPEY, the rock of Craigellachie, and TELFORD'S single span iron BRIDGE. The distillery uses local spring water running from little CONVAL HILL for making MALT SCOTCH WHISKY of light and smoky character.

AGED 14 YEARS

43% vol   70cl

• AGE •

14 years

• STRENGTH •

43%

• TASTE RATING •

3

• COMMENTS •

*A smoky-smelling and
tasting malt of medium body,
Craigellachie works well
as an after-dinner dram.*

• VISITORS •

*The distillery is not open
to visitors.*

This distillery is pleasantly situated
on high ground above the River
Spey outside Dufftown. It was
built in 1891 by the Craigellachie
Distillery Co., a founder of which
was Peter Mackie, the creator of the
White Horse brand. Mackie and Co.
(later White Horse Distillers) subsequently bought the distillery in
1915. It was owned by United
Distillers (later Diageo) but was
sold in 1998 to Bermuda-based
drinks giant Bacardi. However, its
single malt is still available under
Diageo's Distillery (Flora and Fauna)
Malts label.

single malt

CRAWFORD'S THREE STAR

Whyte & Mackay Ltd, Glasgow

• STRENGTH •

40%

• TASTE RATING •

2

• COMMENTS •

A smooth, nicely balanced blend with light, malty flavours.

A. & A. Crawford was established in 1860 as a Leith-based whisky merchant and blenders, but it was the founders' sons who launched the successful Crawford's Three Star blend at the start of the twentieth century. The de luxe Five Star appeared in the 1920s and was also well received. The company was acquired by the Distillers Company Ltd in 1944 and ownership subsequently passed to Whyte & Mackay in 1986. Whyte & Mackay Ltd was the subject of a management buy-out in 2001.

CUTTY SARK

Berry Brothers & Rudd Ltd, London

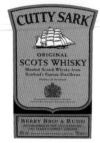

A delicate, smooth whisky with a fresh, crisp taste. A high proportion of oak-matured Speyside malts contributes greatly to its smooth taste.

Berry Brothers & Rudd, London wine and spirit merchants since the seventeenth century, launched the Cutty Sark blend in 1923 specifically for the American market. It quickly became a brand leader, a position it has sustained ever since. It is also a leading premium blend in countries as far apart as Greece, Japan, Portugal, Korea and Brazil. The whisky's name comes from a famous clipper built in Scotland in 1869, and the distinctive yellow label was designed by the renowned Scottish artist, James McBey. Cutty Sark also produce a de luxe 12 Years Old of character.

blend

SPEYSIDE
SINGLE MALT *SCOTCH WHISKY*

DAILUAINE

is the GAELIC for "the green vale". The *distillery* established
in 1852, lies in a hollow by the *CARRON BURN* in *BANFFSHIRE*. This
single Malt Scotch Whisky has a full-bodied fruity nose and a smoky finish.
For more than a *hundred years* all *distillery supplies* were despatched by
rail. The steam locomotive "DAILUAINE NO.1" was in use
from 1924–1967 and is preserved on the *STRATHSPEY RAILWAY*.

AGED 16 YEARS

43% vol   Distilled & Bottled in SCOTLAND   DAILUAINE DISTILLERY, Carron, Banffshire, Scotland   70 cl

DAILUAINE

**Dailuaine Distillery,
Carron, Banffshire**

• AGE •

16 years

• STRENGTH •

43%

• TASTE RATING •

4

• COMMENTS •

*This is a rare malt, with a
heathery and sweetish flavour.*

• VISITORS •

*The distillery is not open
to visitors.*

Dailuaine Distillery stands near the Spey below Ben Rinnes and was established in 1851 by William Mackenzie; his son, Thomas, took over and greatly expanded it during the 1880s. Dailuaine was one of a number of distilleries owned by the Dailuaine–Talisker Distillery Co., an amalgamated company formed by Mackenzie. Its current owners are Diageo and most of its produce goes into their blends, such as Johnnie Walker. The single malt features in the Distillery (Flora and Fauna) Malts series.

DALLAS DHU

**Dallas Dhu Distillery,
Forres, Moray**

• AGE •

Varies

• STRENGTH •

40%

• TASTE RATING •

2–3

• COMMENTS •

Medium-bodied and slightly fruity, finishing sweet. Available only from independent bottlers.

• VISITORS •

*Visitors are welcome
0930–1830 daily Apr.–Sept.;
0930–1630 Sat., Mon.–Thurs.
(Thurs. am only) &
1400–1630 Sun.
Visit the Historic Scotland
website:
www.historic-scotland.gov.uk*

Dallas Dhu was built in 1899 to supply malt for Glasgow-based Wright & Greig's Roderick Dhu blend, popular in the Empire at that time. It was later bought by Benmore Distilleries and joined the Distillers Company in 1929 before being mothballed the next year. Production barely restarted when a fire burned down the stillhouse in 1939, but the distillery reopened after the war. After its final closure in 1992, Dallas Dhu was bought by Historic Scotland and reopened as a living monument and example of how a distillery was run a century ago.

THE
DALMORE

SINGLE
HIGHLAND MALT
SCOTCH WHISKY

AGED 12 YEARS

70cl e   40%vol

WHYTE & MACKAY DISTILLERS
GLASGOW G2 5RG
SCOTLAND

THE DALMORE

Dalmore Distillery, Alness, Ross-shire

• AGE •
12 years

• STRENGTH •
40%

• TASTE RATING •
4

• COMMENTS •
A smooth, full-bodied whisky with a hint of sherry and peat in its malted flavours. A good digestif.

• VISITORS •
Visitors are welcome by appointment Mon.–Fri. mid-Aug.– mid-Dec. and mid-Jan.–end June. Telephone 01344-882362 to arrange.

Built in 1839, Dalmore was bought in 1867 by the Mackenzie family. Ownership now rests with Whyte & Mackay Ltd, and much of its produce goes into their blends, including Whyte & Mackay, Stewarts and Claymore. The distillery is attractively set in a picturesque location with a wooded, hilly backdrop and outlook over the Cromarty Firth to the fertile Black Isle. Its location brought a break in the production of whisky during the First World War when the American navy took over the distillery and its access to the deep-water Cromarty Firth, for the manufacture of mines.

DALWHINNIE

**Dalwhinnie Distillery,
Dalwhinnie, Inverness-shire**

• AGE •
15 years

• STRENGTH •
43%

• TASTE RATING •
2–3

• COMMENTS •
Ideal as a pre- or post-dinner dram, Dalwhinnie is light and aromatic with a soft, heather-honey finish.

• VISITORS •
*Visitors are welcome 0930–1630 Mon.–Fri., Mar.–Dec.
Hours extended in summer, restricted in winter.
Telephone 01528-522208.*

Built in 1898 at the end of the boom years for the whisky industry, what is today Dalwhinnie Distillery was called Strathspey when it first opened, even though it was not, strictly speaking, on Speyside. It stands on the Drumochter Pass at a height of more than 1000 feet, close to pure water sources, and for was many years Scotland's highest distillery. It is presently owned by Diageo. Most of its output went to blending until 1988 when the Dalwhinnie single malt was developed.

single malt

DEANSTON

Deanston Distillery, Doune, Stirlingshire

• AGE •

12, 17 years

• STRENGTH •

40%

• TASTE RATING •

2–3

• COMMENTS •

A medium-bodied and smooth Highland malt with a sweetish, fruity flavour.

• VISITORS •

The distillery is not open to visitors.

Originally a cotton mill dating from 1785, Deanston was converted to a whisky distillery in 1966. Water for distilling and electricity comes from the River Teith that rises north of Loch Lomond and flows through the Trossachs. The mill's original weaving sheds, with their humidity control and their temperature, are perfect for maturing the whisky and are considered to add a natural smoothness to its character. Deanston was bought by Burn Stewart of Glasgow in 1991.

DEWAR'S WHITE LABEL

**Diageo,
Banbeath, Leven, Fife**

• STRENGTH •
40%

• TASTE RATING •
2

• COMMENTS •

*Dewar's White Label, the
best-selling Scotch whisky
in the USA, has a slightly
smoky aroma and a complex,
delicate, malty flavour with
a clean, dry finish.*

Founded in Perth in 1846, John Dewar and Sons was a major success story of the Scottish whisky industry. The company pioneered the development of new export markets: first to sell its whisky in bottles (so opening up new markets in the home); and quick to grasp the importance of advertising – Dewar's was among the first companies whose bottles bore its company name. By the time it became part of the Distillers Company Ltd in 1925, it owned seven distilleries. More than 90% of production is exported.

blend

DIMPLE

**Diageo,
Banbeath, Leven, Fife**

• AGE •

15 years

• STRENGTH •

40%

• TASTE RATING •

2–3

• COMMENTS •

Dimple is the de luxe whisky from Haig, a family associated with the whisky industry for almost three and a half centuries. They were innovators in the industry in the nineteenth century, and were acquired by the Distillers Company in 1919. Today Haig holds the licence for three malt distilleries: Glenkinchie, Glenlossie and Mannochmore, as well as Cameronbridge grain distillery in Fife. Diageo own the Dimple brand.

Dimple, in its distinctive triangular bottle, is a good quality de luxe blend which is also a leader in its market in the UK. More sophisticated than the standard Haig blend, it has a mellow sweetness which is harmoniously balanced by a smoky, peaty flavour.

de luxe

DRAMBUIE

**Drambuie,
Kirkliston, West Lothian**

Prince Charles Edwards Liqueur

DRAMBUIE

This Ancient and delicate Liqueur was prepared in Skye
when the Recipe was first brought to Scotland in 1745

• STRENGTH •
40%

• TASTE RATING •
2

• COMMENTS •
*Based on a blend of secret
ingredients, Drambuie is a
sweet after-dinner whisky
liqueur with a rich and creamy
honeyed flavour complemented
by fragrant, fruity notes.*

• VISITORS •
*The plant is not open
to visitors.*

Drambuie is produced in the Lothians, having moved from its original home on Skye a century ago. Drambuie ('the drink that satisfies') is said to have been the personal liqueur of Prince Charles Edward Stuart, Bonnie Prince Charlie. After his army's defeat by the Hanoverians at Culloden in 1746, the prince fled to Skye with a few supporters. Among them was Captain John Mackinnon, a native of Skye whom, so the story goes, the prince rewarded for his loyalty by giving him his only remaining possession – the secret recipe for his personal liqueur.

DRUMGRAY HIGHLAND CREAM LIQUEUR

Burn Stewart, Glasgow

• STRENGTH •

17%

• TASTE RATING •

2

• COMMENTS •

A light cream liqueur with Deanston single malt as its base and complemented by sweet herbal notes.

Drumgray Highland Cream complements Wallace, Burn Stewart's single malt liqueur, and the company's whisky portfolio which includes a range of malts from Tobermory and Deanston distilleries. Burn Stewart were bought in December 2002 by CL Financial, an overseas company with other interests in the drinks industry. Several of Burn Stewart's products, including Drumgray (named 'Best Cream Liqueur in the World'), have won medals in international competition.

DUFFTOWN

**Dufftown Distillery,
Dufftown, Keith, Banffshire**

• AGE •

15 years

• STRENGTH •

43%

• TASTE RATING •

2–3

• COMMENTS •

*A pleasant Speyside malt
with a delicate, fragrant aroma
which is almost flowery,
and a smooth, sweet taste.
Doubles as a before- or
after-dinner dram.*

• VISITORS •

*The distillery is not open
to visitors.*

HIGHLAND
SINGLE MALT *SCOTCH WHISKY*

DUFFTOWN

*distillery was established near Dufftown at the end of the (19th) The
bright flash of the KINGFISHER can often be seen over the DULLAN
RIVER, which flows past the old stone buildings of the distillery on
its way north to the SPEY. This single HIGHLAND MALT WHISKY
is typically SPEYSIDE in character with a delicate, fragrant,
almost flowery aroma and taste which lingers on the palate.*

43% vol   AGED 15 YEARS   70cl

Prettily situated at the water's edge
in the Dullan Glen, this is one of
seven distilleries in and around
Dufftown, a major whisky-production
centre with plentiful resources of
water, peat and, once, barley. Despite
the abundance of fresh water in
the glen, there were disputes in
the early years over water rights,
some of which led to the nocturnal
diversion and re-diversion of local
supplies. This distillery finally gained
the right to draw its supplies from
Jock's Well, a reliable source of fine,
sweet water some distance away.

DUNHILL OLD MASTER

Justerini & Brooks, London

• STRENGTH •

43%

• TASTE RATING •

3

• COMMENTS •

Justerini & Brooks was started in London in 1749 by Italian wine merchant Giacomo Justerini; thirty years later he began selling Scotch whisky. In 1962 the company combined with W. & A. Gilbey to form International Distillers and Vintners Ltd (IDV); they were in turn bought by Grand Metropolitan ten years later. J&B have created a range of high-quality premium whiskies for Alfred Dunhill Ltd, including Dunhill Centenary, Dunhill's Celebration Edition and Dunhill's Gentlemen's Speyside blend.

A combination of over thirty individual whiskies, some more than twenty years old, Dunhill Old Master is an exceptionally smooth, richly flavoured blend. Old Master is the standard Dunhill blend.

blend

FAIRLIE'S LIGHT HIGHLAND LIQUEUR

**Glenturret Distillery,
The Hosh, Perthshire**

• AGE •
12 years

• STRENGTH •
24%

• TASTE RATING •
2

• COMMENTS •

Smooth and delicate without being cloying the secret recipe used to produce this unique drink allows the top-grade malt used to come through. Excellent as a mixer.

• VISITORS •

Visitors are welcome to The Famous Grouse Experience at Glenturret Distillery all year round. Telephone 01764-656565 or 08450-451800.

Fairlie's Light Highland Liqueur is produced at Glenturret Distillery, situated in one of Perthshire's most spectacular Highland settings. It is named after the family which did so much to resurrect the distillery's fortunes in the 1960s. The label sports a pouncing cat motif and paw prints in honour of the late Towser, the distillery's famous cat whose record of 28,899 mice caught in a twenty-four year career earned her a place in the *Guinness Book of Records* as the world's most successful mouser.

liqueur

THE FAMOUS GROUSE

FINEST SCOTCH WHISKY

A marriage of the rare Scotch whiskies

PERTH

40% vol   Matthew Gloag & Son Ltd., Perth, Scotland   70cl
PRODUCT OF SCOTLAND

THE FAMOUS GROUSE

Matthew Gloag and Son, Perth, Perthshire

• AGE •
12 years

• STRENGTH •
40%

• TASTE RATING •
3

• COMMENTS •
The Famous Grouse is a light-to-medium-bodied whisky with a fresh smoothness and a pleasant, lightly peated flavour. It has been the most popular blend in Scotland for several years.

• VISITORS •
Visitors are welcome to The Famous Grouse Experience at Glenturret Distillery all year round. Telephone 01764-656565 or 08450-451800.

Matthew Gloag began in Perth in 1800 as a licensed grocers, acquiring blending and bottling interests as the firm expanded during the nineteenth century. What was to become their most famous product appeared in 1895, with the grouse on the name and label successfully capitalizing on the popularity of game shooting among the Victorians and Edwardians. The company was bought by Highland Distilleries in 1970 and received the benefits of wider distribution and advertising to become one of the most popular blends in its home country.

FRASER McDONALD

Gibson Scotch Whisky Ltd, Glasgow

40%

2–3

Fraser McDonald is a smooth and mellow blend whose light, fresh taste is underlain by gentle peaty notes.

Fraser McDonald is the standard blend of Gibson Scotch Whisky Distilleries Ltd, a subsidiary of Loch Lomond Distillery Co. Ltd of Alexandria. As well as a new grain complex at Loch Lomond, the company holds two malt distilleries: Loch Lomond at Alexandria, and Glen Scotia in Campbeltown. Fiercely-independent, the company is free of the constraints of the corporate giants and continues to develop its own unique position in the industry.

GLAYVA

**Glayva Liqueur,
Leith, Edinburgh**

• AGE •

12 years

• STRENGTH •

35%

• TASTE RATING •

2

• COMMENTS •

Glayva was originally created by Ronald Morrison and Co., an Edinburgh merchants well versed in flavours and bouquets. The combination of aged whisky, syrup of herbs, aromatic oils and honey took many years to perfect. Ownership of Glayva passed to Whyte & Mackay in 1993 when they acquired Invergordon Distillers, owners of the brand since 1984. Whyte & Mackay were bought out by an in-house consortium in 2002. Glayva is one of the biggest sellers in the Scotch whisky liqueur market.

Glayva, whose name derives from the Gaelic for 'very good', is a rich, syrupy-textured after-dinner liqueur with a hint of tangerine in its sweet flavours.

• VISITORS •

The plant is not open to visitors.

GLENBURGIE

The Glenburgie-Glenlivet Distillery, Forres, Moray

SINGLE HIGHLAND MALT

GLENBURGIE

TRADE MARK OF PROPRIETORS: J G STODART LTD

SCOTCH WHISKY

40% VOL   AGED 8 YEARS   70cl

PRODUCT OF SCOTLAND

*SPECIALLY SELECTED, PRODUCED AND
BOTTLED AT AND UNDER THE RESPONSIBILITY OF*
GORDON & MACPHAIL
ELGIN, SCOTLAND. REGD. BOTTLER.

* AGE *

Varies; 10 years

* STRENGTH *

Varies

* TASTE RATING *

3

* COMMENTS *

A light-bodied, delicate single malt whose sweet, slightly floral taste makes it ideal as an aperitif. It is found relatively rarely in this country, as most goes for export.

* VISITORS *

The distillery has no reception centre but visitors are welcome by appointment. Telephone 01343-850258 to arrange.

A distillery was said to have been established here in 1810, but production ceased and was not revived until the second half of the nineteenth century. It was bought by James & George Stodart Ltd of Dumbarton who themselves were taken over by Hiram Walker in the 1930s. The distillery was extended in 1958 and is now owned by Allied Distillers, with most of its produce going into their blends. A 10 Year Old is due for release before the end of 2003.

single malt

GLENCADAM

**Glencadam Distillery,
Brechin, Angus**

Varies

Varies

3–4

*An excellent and well-rounded
dram with a fruit-salad nose
and sticky toffee pudding
flavour. Glencadam is generally
available from independent
whisky merchants.*

*The distillery has no
reception centre but visitors
are welcome by appointment.
Telephone 01356-622217
to arrange.*

Glencadam, built around 1825, dates around the time of the first wave of licensed distilleries, and was one of two in Brechin dating from this decade (North Port being the other). It takes its water from Moorfoot Loch. It was sold by Allied Distillers to Angus Dundee in 2002 and production restarted. Although its produce is only available from independent bottlers, its new owners plan to launch two single malts, an 8 Years Old and a 15 Years Old, in 2004. Glencadam is presently the only working distillery in Angus.

GLEN CALDER

**Gordon and MacPhail,
Elgin, Moray**

40%

2

*A very pleasant blend with a
smooth, honey-like nose and
light, slightly smoky finish.*

*Gordon and MacPhail's shop,
South St, Elgin is open
0900–1715 Mon., Tues. & Fri.;
0900–1700 Wed. & Sat.;
0830–1715 Thurs.
Telephone 01343-545110.*

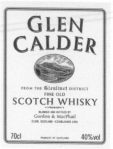

GLEN
CALDER

FROM THE Glenlivet DISTRICT
FINE OLD
SCOTCH WHISKY
BLENDED AND BOTTLED BY
Gordon & MacPhail
ELGIN, SCOTLAND • ESTABLISHED 1895

70cl   PRODUCT OF SCOTLAND   40%vol

Gordon and MacPhail started in
business in 1895 as a licensed grocer
and wine and spirit merchant, as had
so many of the foremost names among
the Scotch whisky blending industry.
Unlike the others, however, Gordon
and MacPhail retained all the original
aspects of their business as well as
extending into vatting, blending,
bottling and, more recently, distilling.
They are today the world's leading
malt whisky specialists. Glen Calder
is an award-winning blend, and one
of the most popular in northern
Scotland.

blend

GLEN DEVERON

**Macduff Distillery,
Banff, Banffshire**

A modern distillery, built in 1960, Macduff is one of the few distilleries to give its single malt a different name from its own (although independent bottlers do market the whisky, including miniatures, under the name of 'Macduff'). The malt takes its name from the nearby River Deveron from which is drawn the water used for cooling in the production process. Macduff Distillery is owned by William Lawson Distillers, a subsidiary of Bacardi Ltd, Bermuda who hold four other distilleries: Aberfeldy, Aultmore, Royal Brackla and Craigellachie.

GLENDRONACH

**The Glendronach Distillery,
Forgue, Huntly,
Aberdeenshire**

The
GLENDRONACH
100% MATURED IN
SHERRY CASKS
Single Highland Malt
Scotch Whisky
AGED 15 YEARS
40% vol   70cl e
BOTTLED IN SCOTLAND

• AGE •

12 years

• STRENGTH •

40%, 43%

• TASTE RATING •

3

• COMMENTS •

*Glendronach is a beautifully
rounded single malt whose
slight peaty tones are balanced
by a lingering sweetness.*

• VISITORS •

*The distillery has two tours daily,
at 1000 and 1400 Mon.–Fri.
The shop is open
0900–1600 Mon.–Fri.
Telephone 01466-730245.*

The distillery, set picturesquely on the
Dronach Burn in the Aberdeenshire
countryside, is one of the most attractive in the Highlands. Built in 1826,
it was one of the first to be licensed,
and its whisky enjoyed a wide repu-
tation in the nineteenth century. Its
original hand-turned malting floor
and coal-fired stills have been retained.
Since 1960 it has been operated by
William Teacher & Sons, with produce
going into the Teacher's blends. Allied
Distillers acquired both blends and
distillery in 1988. They restarted
production in 2002 after the distillery
was mothballed for six years.

SPEYSIDE
SINGLE MALT
SCOTCH WHISKY

GLENDULLAN

distillery, located in a beautiful wooded valley was ⅞ built in 1897 and is one of seven established in Dufftown in the C19th. The River Fiddich flows past the distillery; originally providing power to drive machinery, it is now used ⅞ for cooling. GLENDULLAN is a firm, mellow single MALT SCOTCH WHISKY with a fruity bouquet and a smooth lingering finish.

AGED **12** YEARS

43% vol   70cl

GLENDULLAN

**Glendullan Distillery,
Dufftown, Keith, Banffshire**

● AGE ●

12 years

● STRENGTH ●

43%

● TASTE RATING ●

3

● COMMENTS ●

A good single malt with a robust character yet a mellow, fruity flavour.

● VISITORS ●

Visitors are welcome by appointment. Telephone 01340-820250 to arrange.

This is one of the seven Dufftown distilleries, built just 100 years ago in a picturesque setting on the banks of the Fiddich. Built for William Williams of Aberdeen, it passed to the control of Macdonald Greenlees & Williams after the First World War and, with its parent company, into the ownership of the Distillers Company Ltd in 1926. It is now owned by Diageo. As well as being bottled as a single malt in the Distillery (Flora and Fauna) Malts series, Glendullan is an important component of Old Parr and of President, a de luxe blend.

GLENFARCLAS

**Glenfarclas Distillery,
Ballindalloch, Banffshire**

• AGE •

*10, 12, 15, 21, 25,
30 years and others*

• STRENGTH •

40%, 43%, 46%, 60%

• TASTE RATING •

3–4, 5 (60%; cask strength)

• COMMENTS •

*Glenfarclas is a whisky of
true character, and is widely
acknowledged as a classic malt.
Whiskies across the range are
characterized by their distinctive,
full-bodied and mellow,
sherried character.*

• VISITORS •

*Visitors are welcome
1000–1730 Mon.–Fri., Apr.–Sept.,
& Sat. June–Sept.;
1000–1600 Mon.–Fri., Oct.–Mar.;
or by appointment.
Last tour one hour before closing.
Telephone 01807-505209
or visit the website:
www.glenfarclas.co.uk*

Glenfarclas is one of the very few independent distilleries left in Scotland. Established in 1836 and purchased in 1865 by John Grant, Glenfarclas Distillery remains firmly in the hands of the Grant family (unrelated to the Grant family at Glenfiddich) under the company name of J. & G. Grant. Glenfarclas bottle a wide selection of single malts at different ages and strengths. The distillery is located in the heart of Speyside beneath the slopes of Ben Rinnes and its well-maintained visitor centre attracts thousands annually from around the world.

single malt

GLENFIDDICH

**Glenfiddich Distillery,
Dufftown, Keith, Banffshire**

• AGE •

12 years

• STRENGTH •

40%

• TASTE RATING •

2

• COMMENTS •

*Glenfiddich has a fresh, fruity
nose and flavour with a hint of
heather and peat. An excellent
introduction to malt whisky,
and ideal, too, as an aperitif.*

Glenfiddich Distillery was started
by William Grant, a former apprentice
shoemaker who worked at Mortlach,
another Dufftown distillery, gaining experience and money enough
to set up on his own in 1887. The
new distillery was successful as
soon as it went into production, and
has remained so ever since, thanks
not only to the quality and accessibility of its product but also to far-
sighted marketing which has made
its single malt one of the best loved
in the world.

• VISITORS •

*The distillery is on the Whisky
Trail and visitors are welcome
0930–1630 Mon.–Fri. all year;
0930–1630 Sat., 1200–1630 Sun.,
Easter–mid Oct. Large parties
must book in advance:
telephone 01340-820373.*

GLEN GARIOCH

**Glengarioch Distillery,
Oldmeldrum, Aberdeenshire**

| • AGE • |
| 10, 15, 21 years |

| • STRENGTH • |
| 40%, 43% |

| • TASTE RATING • |
| 3 |

| • COMMENTS • |

*This medium-bodied whisky,
with hints of lavender and
oak and a syrupy sweetness,
is an ideal after-dinner dram.*

Set in the Aberdeenshire market
town of Oldmeldrum, Glengarioch
established in 1797. It has had several
owners throughout its history, and
was sold by the Distillers Company
Ltd in 1970 to Morrison Bowmore,
two years after its closure because of
a shortage of water. Having sunk a
new well, Morrison were able to tap
sufficient sources of spring water
to enable normal production to continue. The distillery was mothballed
in 1995 but opened again in 1997.

single malt

GLENGOYNE

Glengoyne Distillery, Dumgoyne, Stirlingshire

• AGE •

10, 17, 21 years

• STRENGTH •

43%

• TASTE RATING •

2–3

• COMMENTS •

A light, pleasant, sweetish whisky with a fragrant aroma and no abrasive edges. Ideal as an aperitif.

• VISITORS •

Visitors are welcome 1000–1600 Mon.–Sat. all year and 1200–1600 Sun., Easter–Oct. Visits by appointment Dec.–Mar. Telephone 01360-550254.

Glengoyne stands just north of the Highland Line (the line initiated by the Customs and Excise to differentiate area boundaries between styles of whisky) and so qualifies as a Highland distillery. It was built in 1833 at the foot of the Campsie Fells, near the fifty-foot waterfall from which it takes its supplies. It was bought by Lang Brothers in 1876 and was sympathetically restored and extended in the 1960s. Ian MacLeod & Co. are current owners of Glengoyne, having bought the distillery from Edrington in 2003.

GLEN GRANT

**Glen Grant Distillery,
Rothes, Moray**

• AGE •

No age, 5, 10 years

• STRENGTH •

40%, 43%

• TASTE RATING •

2

• COMMENTS •

*The 5 Years Old is light and dry,
making it ideal as an aperitif,
while the older version has
a sweeter, fruitier, more
rounded character.*

• VISITORS •

*Visitors are welcome
1000–1600 Mon.–Sat.,
Sun 1230–1600
Apr.–Oct. inclusive .
Telephone 01340-832118.*

Opened by James and John Grant in
1840, Glen Grant enjoyed continuous
expansion throughout the last century and this has continued to the
present day. James Grant, known as
'The Mayor' was only 25 when he set
about achieving his vision of pure
malt with a clear colour. Its unique
flavour and appearance is due to the
purifiers and tall slenders stills James
Grant designed and his decision to
retain its natural colour. The distillery
is now owned by Chivas Brothers,
the Scotch whisky business of
Pernod Ricard.

GLEN KEITH

**Glen Keith Distillery,
Keith, Banffshire**

• AGE •

Varies

• STRENGTH •

40%

• TASTE RATING •

2–3

• COMMENTS •

*A medium-bodied, fruity malt,
smoky and chocolatey on the
palate with a dry finish.*

Glen Keith was built by Chivas
Brothers in 1958, across the River Isla
from Strathisla, another of their distilleries and one of the oldest in
Scotland. As if by deliberate contrast,
processes used at Glen Keith were
innovative, and it was the first of the
Scotch whisky distilleries to have its
production processes automated.
Unlike the usual practice, distillations
were not bottled at fixed ages but
were individually selected at what
was judged to be the optimum point
in the maturation process. Owners
Pernod Ricard mothballed Glen Keith
after they acquired Chivas in 1999.

GLENKINCHIE

**Glenkinchie Distillery,
Pencaitland, Tranet,
East Lothian**

• AGE •
10 years

• STRENGTH •
43%

• TASTE RATING •
3

• COMMENTS •

*Ideal as an aperitif,
Glenkinchie, the Edinburgh
malt, is the driest and smokiest
of Lowland whiskies. It is a
fine, pale, smooth whisky.*

• VISITORS •

*Visitors are welcome
0930–1700 Mon.–Fri.,
1200–1700 Sat., June– Oct.
Restricted hours Nov.–May.
Telephone 01875-342004.*

Glenkinchie takes its name from the burn which flows by it and the glen in which it stands. It was established in the late 1830s and has been in production since, except during the wars. The licence is held by Haig, the brand owned by Diageo, and most of Glenkinchie's product goes into their blends. The single malt was also bottled by Diageo in their Classic Malts series.

THE
GLENLIVET.

George Smith's Original 1824
Pure Single Malt
Scotch Whisky

AGED 12 YEARS

Aged only in Oak Casks

GEORGE & J. G. SMITH

Distilled in Scotland at
The Glenlivet Distillery, Banffshire

PRODUCT OF SCOTLAND

70cl 700ml e 40%vol 40°Gl 40% alc./vol.

THE GLENLIVET

The Glenlivet Distillery, Ballindalloch, Banffshire

• AGE •
12, 18, 21 years

• STRENGTH •
40%, 43%

• TASTE RATING •
3–4

• COMMENTS •
The Glenlivet is a subtly balanced malt. Its light, delicate bouquet has traces of fruit, and floral notes, while the complex flavours are delicately balanced between a medium sweetness and smooth dryness.

• VISITORS •
Visitors are welcome 1000–1600 Mon.–Sat., Sun. 1230–1600 Apr.– Oct. inclusive. Telephone 01340-832157.

This was one of the first distilleries licensed under the reforming 1823 Licensing Act – a fact which so incensed his still-illegal neighbours that its founder, George Smith, was obliged to carry pistols for his own protection. The whisky so grew in popularity that other distillers adopted the name, and an ensuing legal case and settlement (which endures to this day) allowed the Smiths to use the direct article in their whisky's name while others were to use it as a hyphenated suffix. The Glenlivet 18 Years Old was a prizewinner in international competition in 2003. The Distillery is now owned by Chivas Brothers, the Scotch whisky business of Pernod Ricard.

single malt

GLENLOCHY

**Glenlochy Distillery,
Fort William, Inverness-shire**

HIGHLAND MALT SCOTCH WHISKY
FROM
**GLENLOCHY
DISTILLERY**

40%vol DISTILLED 1965 ~ BOTTLED 2002 70cl

SPECIALLY SELECTED, PRODUCED & BOTTLED BY GORDON & MACPHAIL, ELGIN, SCOTLAND

• AGE •

40%

• STRENGTH •

Varies

• TASTE RATING •

2

• COMMENTS •

*A malt with a strong sherry
influence with spices and
floral notes, finishing
surprisingly smoky.*

Glenlochy Distillery was built close to
Loch Lochy at the southern end of the
Caledonian Canal in a pretty setting
on the outskirts of Fort William. It was
built in 1900 with production beginning the following year. The single
malt product is now something of a
rarity, as the distillery was closed by
its parent company, United Distillers,
in the 1980s, and sold outside the
industry in 1991.

single malt

SPEYSIDE
SINGLE MALT SCOTCH WHISKY

The three spirit stills at the

GLENLOSSIE

distillery have *purifiers* installed between the *lyne arm* and the
condenser. This has a bearing on the character of the single
MALT SCOTCH WHISKY produced which has a fresh, grassy
aroma and a smooth, lingering flavour. Built in 1876 by John Duff,
the distillery lies four miles south of ELGIN in Morayshire.

AGED 10 YEARS

43% vol   70 cl

GLENLOSSIE

**Glenlossie-Glenlivet
Distillery,
Birnie, Elgin, Moray**

• AGE •

10 years

• STRENGTH •

43%

• TASTE RATING •

2

• COMMENTS •

*Not the easiest of whiskies
to find, Glenlossie has a fresh,
grassy aroma with a touch
of fruitiness and a smooth,
lingering flavour.*

• VISITORS •

*Visitors are welcome
by appointment.
Telephone 01343-86331
to arrange.*

Glenlossie was built not far from
the River Lossie in 1876 by a former
distillery manager-turned-hotel
owner from Lhanbryde, near Elgin.
It was expanded and improved
between 1896 and 1917. In 1962, its
stills were increased from four to
six, while in 1992 a new mash tun
was fitted. The licensee is presently
Haig and the distillery is owned by
Diageo who bottle it in their Distillery
(Flora and Fauna) Malts series.

single malt

GLEN MHOR

**Glen Mhor Distillery,
Inverness, Inverness-shire**

• AGE •
Varies

• STRENGTH •
40%

• TASTE RATING •
3

• COMMENTS •
*A complex, malty whisky,
smoky and fruity on the palate,
finishing oaky and smoky.*

This distillery was built between 1892 and 1894 by Mackinlay and Birnie who were later to own the neighbouring Glen Albyn Distillery; John Birnie had previously managed Glen Albyn. Glen Mhor used the same water (from Loch Ness) and peat as its neighbour, but their whiskies were quite different. It was one of the first distilleries in Scotland to introduce mechanical malting in the late 1940s. It was also one of the Scottish Malt Distillers distilleries closed down by the Distillers Company Ltd in 1983 and was demolished in 1988.

single malt

GLENMORANGIE

**Glenmorangie Distillery,
Tain, Ross-shire**

• AGE •

10, 18 years

• STRENGTH •

40%, 43%

• TASTE RATING •

3–4

• COMMENTS •

*A smooth and medium bodied
whisky, with a delicate, slightly
sweet aroma. Scotland's
best-selling single malt.*

• VISITORS •

*Visitors are welcome
0900–1700 Mon.–Fri. all year
and at weekends, June–Aug.
Phone for details.
Telephone 01862-892477
to arrange.*

Distilling was begun here in 1843 by the Mathieson family as a sideline to farming. In 1918, The Glenmorangie Distillery Company passed into the control of its present owners, Macdonald and Muir Ltd. Water is supplied by unusually hard, mineral-rich springs in nearby Tarlogie Forest, and the lightly peated new spirit is distilled in Glenmorangie's characteristically tall, swan-necked stills, before being transferred into charred American oak barrels for the maturation process.

single malt

GLEN MORAY

**Glen Moray Distillery,
Elgin, Moray**

• AGE •
12, 16 years

• STRENGTH •
40%, 43%

• TASTE RATING •
2–3

• COMMENTS •

*Golden in colour, with a soft,
fresh bouquet leading into a
smooth and rounded taste,
Glen Moray is a classic
Speyside malt.*

• VISITORS •

*Visitors are welcome
by appointment.
Tours 0900–1700 Mon.–Fri.
Also 1000–1600 Sat., June–Sept.
Telephone 01343-542577
to arrange.*

Established during the whisky boom
years of the 1890s, the Glen Moray
Distillery was expanded in 1958. It is
owned by Macdonald & Muir Ltd, and,
in addition to its availability as a single
malt, its produce also features in many
well-known blends. Glen Moray is the
sister distillery to the better known
Glenmorangie.

GLEN ORD

**Glen Ord Distillery,
Muir of Ord, Ross-shire**

• AGE •
12 years

• STRENGTH •
40%

• TASTE RATING •
2–3

• COMMENTS •
*A smooth, well-rounded,
slightly dry malt with a
fragrant bouquet and
mellow finish.*

• VISITORS •
*Visitors are welcome
0930–1700 Mon.–Fri., Mar.–Oct.
Weekend opening July–Sept.;
restricted hours Nov.–Feb.
Telephone 01463-872004.*

This distillery is set in an area which was infamous for illicit distillation even as late as a century ago. It stands on a tributary of the River Conan, the Oran Burn, whose clear waters have been used by legal and illegal whisky producers alike. Ord Distillery, as it then was, was founded in 1838 on land leased from the Mackenzies of Ord to provide a ready market for barley produced on Mackenzie farms. It was acquired by Dewar in 1923, and is now owned by Diageo.

single malt

GLEN ROSA

Isle of Arran Distillery, Lochranza, Isle of Arran

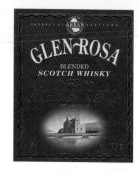

• STRENGTH •
40%

• TASTE RATING •
2

• COMMENTS •

A medium-dry whisky with soft, sweet aromas and a rich, smooth, vanilla-sweetness in its flavour and a malty note to its finish.

• VISITORS •

Visitors are welcome at the award-winning visitor centre. Tours are held daily. 1000–1800, mid-Mar.–end Oct. Reduced opening hours in Nov. and Dec.; telephone 01770-830264 for details.

Isle of Arran Distillers are a dynamic and independent new player in the Scotch whisky industry. Their distillery on Arran at Lochranza opened in 1995 and the company now successfully markets its portfolio of blends and malts throughout Europe, Asia and the American continent. The company's new malt, The Arran Malt, has been acclaimed by whisky writers around the world.

blend

THE GLENROTHES

**Glenrothes Distillery,
Rothes, Moray**

The Glenrothes Distillery was built in 1878 for William Grant & Sons with the backing of a group of local businessmen, including the provost of Rothes. It was bought in 1887 by the Islay Distillery Company, owners of Bunnahabhain, and became part of the Highland Distilleries company. The distillery has been expanded twice in the last 30 years. The Glenrothes Vintage single malt is produced and distributed by Berry Brothers & Rudd, the owners of Cutty Sark whisky, in which Glen Rothes also features.

• AGE •

Varies

• STRENGTH •

43%

• TASTE RATING •

3–4

• COMMENTS •

A popular, full-bodied single malt with a delicate, lightly peated aroma, and a pleasingly sweet, smooth aftertaste.

• VISITORS •

The distillery is not open to visitors.

GLEN SCOTIA

**Glen Scotia Distillery,
Campbeltown, Argyllshire**

• AGE •

12 years

• STRENGTH •

40%

• TASTE RATING •

3

• COMMENTS •

*Glen Scotia is a rich, peaty, oily
malt with a pungent aroma and
a smooth, well-rounded finish.*

• VISITORS •

*Glen Scotia can accommodate
visitors by prior arrangement.
For more information, visit:
www.lochlomonddistillery.com*

Scotia, as it was previously known,
was one of thirty-two Campbeltown
distilleries operating last century,
although only two now remain. Glen
Scotia was built in 1835 and has had
many owners over the years, the
ghost of one of whom is said to haunt
the place. The distillery is now operated by Loch Lomond Distilleries Ltd,
who restarted production in 1999
after the distillery was mothballed.

single malt

GLENTAUCHERS

**Glentauchers Distillery,
Mulben, Banffshire**

• AGE •

Varies

• STRENGTH •

40%

• TASTE RATING •

2

• COMMENTS •

*The sweetness of Glentauchers'
aroma and taste are balanced
by the light dryness of its finish.
A nice pre-dinner dram, but
generally available only from
independent merchants.*

• VISITORS •

*The distillery has no
reception centre but visitors
are welcome by appointment.
Telephone 01542-860272
to arrange.*

Glentauchers was built in 1898 by
James Buchanan, the entrepreneur
responsible for the success of Black &
White whisky, and its product went
into their blends. Buchanan's distillery
was largely rebuilt and modernized
in 1965 but was silent for a number
of years in the 1980s until Allied
Distillers acquired it from United
Distillers in 1988 and immediately
reopened it

THE GLENTURRET

**Glenturret Distillery,
The Hosh, Crieff, Perthshire**

• AGE •

12, 15, 18, 21, 25 years

• STRENGTH •

40%

• TASTE RATING •

3–4

• COMMENTS •

*Glenturret is an award-winning,
full-bodied Highland malt with
a rich, nutty flavour and nicely
rounded finish.*

• VISITORS •

*Visitors are welcome to
The Famous Grouse Experience
at Glenturret Distillery
all year round.
Telephone 01764-656565
or 08450-451800.*

Glenturret stands in a lovely position on the banks of the River Turret, in an area where smuggling and illicit distillation were rife in the past. It is probable that the distillery's own eighteenth-century origins lie there. Glenturret was closed from the 1920s until 1959, when it was largely rebuilt, anticipating the huge upswing in demand for blended whiskies in the 1960s. Facilities for visitors are among the best of any distillery.

single malt

THE GLENTURRET
ORIGINAL MALT LIQUEUR

**Glenturret Distillery,
The Hosh, Crieff, Perthshire**

The Glenturret Original Malt Liqueur is produced at Scotland's oldest working distillery, officially established in 1775 but with a history predating this by some sixty years. Glenturret Distillery stands in a lovely position on the banks of the River Turret, in an area where smuggling and illicit distillation were rife in the past. Glenturret was closed from the 1920s until 1959, when it was largely rebuilt and its fortunes restored under the direction of the Fairlie family.

• STRENGTH •

35%

• TASTE RATING •

2

• COMMENTS •

*A blend of herbs and
The Glenturret single malt
produce a smooth, delicately
flavoured drink that can be
enjoyed on its own or as
a base for mixers.*

• VISITORS •

*Visitors are welcome to
The Famous Grouse Experience
at Glenturret Distillery
all year round.
Telephone 01764-656565
or 08450-451800.*

GLENURY ROYAL

Glenury Royal Distillery, Stonehaven, Kincardineshire

• AGE •
Varies

• STRENGTH •
40%

• TASTE RATING •
2–3

• COMMENTS •
A golden whisky, floral and slightly smoky with a clean nutty and peaty finish.

Glenury was built in the coastal resort town of Stonehaven by a local MP, Robert Barclay, in 1825. Through his links with William IV's court he gained permission to add the suffix 'Royal' to his distillery. The Distillers Company Limited acquired it in 1953, expanding and rebuilding in 1966. Nearby Cowie water kept the distillery supplied. Glenury was closed in 1985 and finally sold off outside the industry in 1992.

single malt

GRAND MACNISH

Macduff International, Glasgow

• AGE •

Standard, 12, 18 years

• STRENGTH •

40%, 43%

• TASTE RATING •

3

• COMMENTS •

A light, smooth blend in which the sweetness of the predominantly Highland whiskies comes through on the finish.

• VISITORS •

The plant is not open to visitors.

Grand Macnish is produced by Macduff International Ltd, an independent Scotch whisky company. The brand was first established by Robert McNish in 1863, the early days of whisky-blending. It is presently available as a standard blend, a 12 Years Old and an 18 Years Old. The company's range also includes the de luxe Islay Mist and Lauder's blends as well as Glenbeg single malt.

WILLIAM GRANT'S FAMILY RESERVE

Girvan Distillery, Girvan, Ayrshire

• STRENGTH •
43%

• TASTE RATING •
2

• COMMENTS •
A traditional yet individual blend of smooth character with a light, fresh taste which incorporates elements of Glenfiddich and The Balvenie.

• VISITORS •
The plant is not open to visitors.

Grants of Glenfiddich, producers of the world's biggest-selling single malt, also produce two blends: William Grant's Family Reserve and Grant's 12 Year Old, the latter a de luxe blend. The company began in 1887 at Glenfiddich, moving into blending and exporting in 1898 after Pattison, blenders and wholesale merchants, and one of Grant's biggest buyers, went bankrupt. In the 1960s the company moved west, building a complex at Girvan in Ayrshire with a grain distillery and blending facilities. Bottling is carried out at Paisley.

blend

HAIG

**Diageo,
Banbeath, Leven, Fife**

*A nicely balanced whisky
with a fragrant aroma,
Haig is smooth and easy
to drink, with a long,
sweet finish.*

Haig is a name long associated with the whisky industry, going back nearly 350 years when Stirlingshire farmer Robert Haig was rebuked by his local kirk session (church court) for distilling whisky on a Sunday. The family had associations with the Steins, another family of Lowland distillers, and the Dublin distillers, the Jamesons. The Haigs were among the first to bring in new practices and machinery, such as the new patent still in the 1830. The company was acquired by the Distillers Company in 1919 and is now owned by Diageo.

blend

HEATHER CREAM

**Inver House Distillers,
Moffat Distillery,
Airdrie, Lanarkshire**

• STRENGTH •

17%

• TASTE RATING •

2

• COMMENTS •

*Heather Cream is a sweet blend
of cream and malt whisky, with
the subtle taste of chocolate,
coconut and a base of Balblair
single malt. It is one of the most
popular of the Scotch whisky
cream liqueurs available today.*

• VISITORS •

*The distillery and plant are
not open to visitors.*

Heather Cream's producers, Inver
House, own five malt distilleries:
Knockdhu (producing An Cnoc),
Speyburn-Glenlivet, Balblair, Pulteney
and Balmenach. Heather Cream is
produced at their complex at Moffat
Distillery on the outskirts of Airdrie;
a converted mill, it also holds a grain
distillery. After a management buy-
out from its parent company in 1988,
Inver House was for many years one of
the few independent, Scottish-owned
companies in the whisky industry,
but the company was taken over by
Pacific Spirits in 2002.

HIGHLAND PARK

Highland Park Distillery, Kirkwall, Orkney

• AGE •

12 years

• STRENGTH •

40%

• TASTE RATING •

3–4

• COMMENTS •

Highland Park is a medium-bodied single malt of character, with a heathery-smoky aroma and peaty flavour with balancing sweet tones.

Highland Park's origins are linked with an illegal bothy which once occupied the site. Its owner was one of whisky's most colourful characters, Magnus Eunson. A church elder by day and smuggler by night, he was not averse to using the church pulpit as a handy hiding place for his illicit distillations. The distillery was founded in 1798 and passed to the Grant family in 1895. Highland Distilleries purchased it in 1937. The different nature of Orcadian peat is said to be a factor in the distinctiveness of the islands' whiskies.

• VISITORS •

Visitors are welcome 1000–1700 Mon.–Fri. Apr.–Oct. and 1200–1700 Sat. & Sun. July–Aug. Tours every 30 minutes. Large groups should book in advance. Hours restricted in winter. Telephone 01856-874619 to arrange and for details of winter opening.

IMMORTAL MEMORY

**Gordon and MacPhail,
Elgin, Moray**

PRODUCT OF SCOTLAND

Immortal
memory

Scotch
Whisky

RARE SELECTED

*Distilled, Blended and Bottled
in Scotland*

GORDON & MACPHAIL, ELGIN, SCOTLAND

40% vol   70cl

• STRENGTH •
40%

• TASTE RATING •
2

• COMMENTS •
A blend which is floral on the nose – perhaps with a hint of parma violets – with a nutty flavour and a warming finish.

• VISITORS •
Gordon and MacPhail's shop, South St, Elgin is open 0900–1715 Mon., Tues. & Fri.; 0900–1700 Wed. & Sat.; 0830–1715 Thurs. Telephone 01343-545110.

Gordon and MacPhail started in business in 1895 as a licensed grocer and wine and spirit merchant, as did so many of the foremost names among the Scotch whisky blending industry. Unlike the others, however, Gordon and MacPhail have retained all the original aspects of their business as well as extending into vatting, blending, bottling and distilling. Immortal Memory won the title of 'Best Blended Whisky in the World' at the 1991 International Wine and Spirit Competition.

blend

IMPERIAL

**Imperial Distillery,
Carron, Moray**

• AGE •

Varies

• STRENGTH •

Varies

• TASTE RATING •

4

• COMMENTS •

A full-bodied malt with bags of character, Imperial contrives to balance a rich sweetness with a lingering smokiness, with a dark demerara rum nose and an intense flavour of smoke and dried fruit. Available from independent merchants.

The patriotically named Imperial Distillery was established in 1897, the year of Queen Victoria's Diamond Jubilee. Its founder was Thomas Mackenzie who was already the owner of Dailuaine and Talisker. All three distilleries were combined under the name of Dailuaine–Talisker Distilleries Ltd. Imperial Distillery was modernized in the mid 1950s. Production was halted temporarily in the 1980s, but was restarted again after Imperial's purchase by Allied Distillers in 1988 only for the distillery to be mothballed once more ten years later.

single malt

INCHGOWER

**Inchgower Distillery,
Buckie, Banffshire**

• **AGE** •

14 years

• **STRENGTH** •

43%

• **TASTE RATING** •

3

• **COMMENTS** •

*A robust, distinctly heavy-
bodied malt with a combination
of nutty, fruity and spicy
aromas, and a hint of
sweetness in its tones.*

• **VISITORS** •

*Visitors are welcome
by appointment.
Telephone 01542-831161.*

Inchgower was moved from Tochineal
by its founder, Alexander Wilson,
to its present site at Rathaven, near
Buckie, to take advantage of the
ready supply of water from the
Letter Burn and the Springs of
Aultmoor. When the original firm
went out of business, the distillery
passed to Buckie Town Council
who sold it to Arthur Bell and Sons
for £1000 in 1938. Most of the
whisky goes into Bell's blends and
the distillery is now owned by
Diageo who also bottle the single
malt in their Distillery (Flora and
Fauna) Malts range.

SINGLE HIGHLAND MALT

SCOTCH WHISKY

Distilled by
THE LOCH LOMOND DISTILLERY
DUNBARTONSHIRE SCOTLAND

70cl e   40%vol
PRODUCT OF SCOTLAND

INCHMURRIN

**Loch Lomond Distillery,
Alexandria, Dunbartonshire**

• AGE •
10 years

• STRENGTH •
40%

• TASTE RATING •
2

• COMMENTS •
A light, clean, light, pre-dinner malt with a fresh, floral note. A Highland malt with a Lowland character.

• VISITORS •
The distillery is not open to visitors.

A relatively recent addition to the ranks of Scotland's distilleries, Loch Lomond Distillery was founded in 1966. Like Glengoyne, it qualifies as being a Highland malt and is situated just to the south of the world-famous loch. A grain distillery now shares the site. Its present owners, Loch Lomond Distillery Co., also took over Glen Scotia Distillery in Campbeltown and has restarted production there.

single malt

INVERLEVEN

**Inverleven Distillery,
Dumbarton, Dunbartonshire**

● AGE ●

12 years

● STRENGTH ●

40%

● TASTE RATING ●

3

● COMMENTS ●

*A relatively smooth Lowland
malt, with a nice balance of
dry and sweet flavours.
Available from independent
whisky merchants only.*

Built in 1938, Inverleven was part of
a modern-looking red-brick plant
that included Dumbarton grain distillery, on the banks of the Leven in
Dumbarton. Its geographical situation put it on the Highland Line (the
line initiated by the Customs and
Excise to differentiate area boundaries between styles of whisky), and
is counted as a Lowland distillery.
Inverleven's owners, Allied Distillers,
closed the distillery permanently in
1991.

single malt

ISLAY MIST

75cl 40% Vol

Deluxe

BLENDED SCOTCH WHISKY

DISTILLED, BLENDED AND BOTTLED IN SCOTLAND
MACDUFF INTERNATIONAL LIMITED

ISLAY MIST

Macduff International, Glasgow

• AGE •

8, 12, 17 years

• STRENGTH •

40%, 43%

• TASTE RATING •

3

• COMMENTS •

This de luxe blend instantly betrays its origins, though as the name suggests, it is mellower in taste than its main component, Laphroaig. Islay Mist is matured in oak casks and is ideal as an introduction for those wishing to sample the delights of the Islay whiskies.

• VISITORS •

The blending and bottling plant is not open to visitors.

The blenders of Islay Mist, Macduff International, are an independent Scotch whisky company. This mellow Islay de luxe blend first made its appearance in 1928 to mark the 21st birthday of Lord Margadale. As well as Islay Mist, their product range includes Lauder's, one of the oldest blends in the Scotch whisky market, as well as Grand Macnish and Strathbeag blends, and Glenbeg single malt.

ISLE OF JURA

**Isle of Jura Distillery,
Craighouse, Jura, Argyllshire**

ISLE OF
JURA
SINGLE MALT
70d e   Scotch Whisky   40% vol

• AGE •
10 years

• STRENGTH •
40%, 43%

• TASTE RATING •
3

• COMMENTS •
*Reminiscent of a Highland malt,
though with a light, clean,
fragrant palate of its own, this
Island malt is ideal as an aperitif.*

• VISITORS •
*Visitors are welcome
by appointment
11 months of the year.
Telephone 01496-820240
to arrange.*

This distillery was first built overlooking the Sound of Jura in 1810, next to a cave where illicit distillation may have been carried on for as long as three centuries. The distillery's machinery and buildings were owned by different individuals, and a dispute between the two led to its closure for over 50 years in 1913. It was effectively redesigned and rebuilt before its reopening in the 1960s. Its current owners are Whyte & Mackay Ltd who acquired it, and four other distilleries, after a management buy-out from previous owners, Whyte & Mackay, a subsidiary of JBB Greater Europe.

ISLE OF SKYE

**Ian MacLeod & Co.,
Broxburn, West Lothian**

• AGE •

8, 12, 21 years

• STRENGTH •

40%

• TASTE RATING •

3

• COMMENTS •

*A quality blend whose peaty
aroma is complemented by an
underlying sweetness and long,
sherried-spice flavours.*

Ian MacLeod & Co., distillers, blenders and bottlers, were established in 1936 and have remained both independent and family-owned ever since. With other interests in the worldwide spirits industry, the company stated its intention to become a major player in the Scotch whisky industry by its purchase in 2003 of Glengoyne Distillery. Isle of Skye 8 Years Old is very popular in the Highlands, and has established itself in recent years as one of the top five bestselling blends in the UK market.

JεB RARE

Justerini and Brooks, London

• AGE •

12 years

• STRENGTH •

40%, 43%

• TASTE RATING •

2

• COMMENTS •

JεB Rare is a smooth, sweet-tasting whisky with a light, fresh character. It is the number one selling Scotch whisky in Europe and number two in the world.

Justerini and Brooks' principal founder, Giacomo Justerini, was a wine merchant from Bologna. Infatuated by an Italian opera singer, he followed her to London; once there, he set up business with George Johnson in 1749 and they began selling Scotch whisky thirty years later. In 1962 the company joined with others to form International Distillers and Vintners Ltd (IDV) who were bought by Grand Metropolitan in 1972. Today JεB is owned by Diageo, and also produces JεB Reserve, a 15-year-old blend, JεB Jet, a de luxe, and JεB Ultima, featuring a blend of 128 whiskies.

blend

JOHNNIE WALKER BLACK LABEL

**Diageo,
Kilmarnock, Ayrshire**

* AGE *

12 years

* STRENGTH *

40%

* TASTE RATING *

2–3

* COMMENTS *

The best-selling de luxe Scotch whisky in the world, it has a special quality of smoothness and a depth of taste and character which linger on the palate.

Like other major operators in the whisky-blending industry, the original Johnnie Walker started out as a licensed grocer in Kilmarnock in 1820. His grandsons created the Black Label and Red Label blends in the early 1900s. His son, Alexander Walker, bought Cardow Distillery in 1893 to ensure a regular supply of malt for their blends. In 1925 the company joined the Distillers Company Ltd who bought the Talisker and Dailuaine distilleries and licensed the former to Walker. Black Label is now owned by Diageo.

JOHNNIE WALKER BLUE LABEL

**Diageo,
Kilmarnock, Ayrshire**

• AGE •

12 years

• STRENGTH •

40%

• TASTE RATING •

2–3

• COMMENTS •

*Blue Label is among the most
exclusive of blended whiskies,
with a subtle and complex
character and a rich,
pleasing flavour.*

Introduced to the UK market in the 1990s, Blue Label and its recently launched sister brand, Gold Label, are the latest additions to the family of Johnnie Walker whiskies. Most of the product is intended to go for export, particularly to Japanese markets. The Johnnie Walker company began as a licensed grocers in the early nineteenth century and is now one of Diageo's major blending names.

de luxe

JOHNNIE WALKER RED LABEL

Diageo, Kilmarnock, Ayrshire

• STRENGTH •

40%

• TASTE RATING •

2

• COMMENTS •

A smooth blend with sweet and dry notes of maltiness and peatiness. Red Label is the world's biggest-selling blended whisky.

The original Red and Black labels were created in the early 1900s by the grandsons of the company's founder, Kilmarnock grocer Johnnie Walker. A Walker's employee, James Stevenson, was instrumental in persuading the government to introduce a minimum period of maturation in bond for whisky, so raising quality standards and doing the industry a major service. In 1925 the company joined the Distillers Company Ltd, and today Diageo own Johnnie Walker Red Label.

KNOCKANDO

**Knockando Distillery,
Knockando, Aberlour,
Banffshire**

Built during the 1890s whisky boom, Knockando is today owned by Diageo. The distillery's name is said to mean 'small black hill', and Knockando itself is set on a hill overlooking the Spey. Knockando is bottled only when it is considered to have reached its peak rather than at a pre-determined age – generally, this is between twelve and fifteen years. The label lists the year of distillation – the 'season' – and the year of bottling. Such season dating recalls the time when Scottish distilleries only distilled during the winter season after the barley harvest.

single malt

LAGAVULIN

**Lagavulin Distillery,
Port Ellen, Islay, Argyllshire**

From at least the 1740s, moonshiners in this area made and smuggled illicit whisky to the mainland, and Lagavulin's history is rooted in these times. The distillery dates officially from the 1810s and Peter Mackie, the main driving force behind the success of White Horse, started his distilling career at Lagavulin; its malt came to feature strongly in his blend. Lagavulin went into partnership with Mackie's company, later the White Horse Company, and the whisky is still used in White Horse blends. Diageo own the distillery.

* AGE *

16 years

* STRENGTH *

43%

* TASTE RATING *

5

* COMMENTS *

A distinctively Islay malt, powerful and demanding, with a dominant aroma and a dry, peaty–smoky flavour complemented by a trace of sweetness.

* VISITORS *

Visitors are welcome by appointment. Telephone 01496-302400 to arrange.

LANGS SUPREME

Lang Brothers Ltd, Glasgow

• AGE •

5 years

• STRENGTH •

40%

• TASTE RATING •

2

• COMMENTS •

A clean-tasting blend which betrays its Lowland origins with no hints of peat. A warm, lightly sweet and sherried aroma and flavour.

Langs is a long-established and well-known blend in the Scotch whisky market. Langs Supreme standard blend and their 12 Years Old blend are both owned by Ian MacLeod & Co., an independent and family-owned company in the whisky industry for almost 70 years. With other interests in the spirits industry, the company stated its intention to become a major player in the Scotch whisky industry by its purchase from Edrington in 2003 of Langs brands and Glengoyne Distillery, so making it a fully inte-grated distiller, blender and bottler.

blend

LAPHROAIG

**Laphroaig Distillery,
Port Ellen, Islay, Argyllshire**

• AGE •

10, 15, 30, 40 years

• STRENGTH •

40%, 43%, up to 57.4%

• TASTE RATING •

5

• COMMENTS •

A robust, full-bodied, classic Islay malt with a trace of seaweed in its strongly peaty flavour.

• VISITORS •

Visitors are welcome by appointment, Aug.–June. Tours 1030 and 1415 Mon.–Thurs. Telephone 01496-302418.

Laphroaig Distillery is set on a bay on Islay's southern shore, and dates back to 1815. It is a traditional distillery and one of the few still to have a hand-turned malting floor. Allied Distillers, its owners, consider the single malt to be the star performer across their portfolio. Laphroaig is one of the top five best-selling whiskies in the world and is also one of the components in Allied's Long John, Ballantine's and Teacher's blends.

LAUDER'S SCOTCH

Macduff International, Glasgow

Macduff International, the blenders of Lauder's, are an independent Scotch whisky company. Lauder's has been in continuous production since 1836, making it one of the oldest brands available on the market. Throughout its long history, Lauder's has won several gold medals in competition both at home and overseas. As well as Lauder's, Macduff International's product range includes the Islay Mist de luxe, plus Glenbeg single malt and Grand Macnish.

LEDAIG

**Tobermory Distillery,
Tobermory, Mull, Argyllshire**

• AGE •

7, 15, 20 years and others

• STRENGTH •

40%

• TASTE RATING •

5

• COMMENTS •

*Full-bodied single malts from
the Tobermory Distillery, the
Ledaig range is characterized by
strongly peaty, smoky flavours.
The 15 and the 20 Year Olds
are both gold medal
competition winners.*

• VISITORS •

*The Visitor Centre and Distillery
Shop are open Mon.–Fri.,
Easter–30 Sept.
Tours can be arranged
at other times in the year.
Telephone 01688-302645.*

What was once Ledaig Distillery is now Tobermory, having changed its name in the 1970s. The distillery is set in a wooded site by the sea and has enjoyed mixed fortunes since it was first established in 1823, having been closed several times, most recently when it was mothballed in the 1980s. But production has now been on-going since its reopening in 1990, and Morrison Bowmore, owners since 1993, have shown their commitment by greatly expanding the range of whiskies produced at the distillery.

LINKWOOD

**Linkwood Distillery,
Elgin, Moray**

SPEYSIDE
SINGLE MALT
SCOTCH WHISKY

LINKWOOD

distillery stands on the River Lossie,
close to ELGIN in Speyside. The distillery
has remained its traditional atmosphere
since its establishment in 1821.

Great care of has always
been taken to safeguard the
character of the whisky which has
remained the same through the
years. Linkwood is one of the
FINEST of Single Malt Scotch Whiskies
available - full bodied with a hint of
sweetness and a slightly smoky aroma.

YEARS **12** OLD

43% vol   70cl

- **AGE**

12 years

- **STRENGTH**

43%

- **TASTE RATING**

4–5

- **COMMENTS**

*Linkwood is widely acclaimed
as one of the best Speyside
malts, having the area's
characteristics in a fine
balance: smoky, and with
a fruity sweetness underlying
its malty tones.*

- **VISITORS**

*Visitors are welcome by
appointment, 0800–1630.
Telephone 01343-547004
to arrange.*

This is one of the most traditional of distilleries despite having been extensively rebuilt three times since its establishment in the 1820s. It is said that equipment was never replaced until absolutely necessary, and even spiders' webs were left in case the change of environment would affect the whisky. Built by a former provost of Elgin, Linkwood has an attractive wooded setting by Linkwood Burn outside the town. Diageo own the distillery and bottle the malt in their Distillery (Flora and Fauna) Malts range.

PRODUCT OF SCOTLAND

LITTLEMILL

Established 1772

SINGLE LOWLAND MALT
SCOTCH WHISKY

DISTILLED AND BOTTLED IN SCOTLAND BY
LITTLEMILL DISTILLERY CO. LTD.
BOWLING, DUNBARTONSHIRE, SCOTLAND

70cl ℮   40%vol

LITTLEMILL

**Littlemill Distillery,
Bowling, Dunbartonshire**

• AGE •

8, 12 years

• STRENGTH •

40%

• TASTE RATING •

2–3

• COMMENTS •

*A light Highland malt with
a smooth, sweet flavour.
Good as an aperitif.*

Littlemill began life as a brewery centuries before distilling was started, with its ale apparently crossing the Clyde to supply the monks of Paisley Abbey. It was established as a distillery in the late eighteenth century and was one of the earliest in Scotland. Its water came from the Kilpatrick Hills, to the north of the Highland Line (the line initiated by the Customs and Excise to differentiate area boundaries between styles of whisky), and Littlemill is classified as a Highland whisky. The distillery is now closed and has been sold out of the industry.

single malt

THE LIVING CASK

**Loch Fyne Whiskies,
Inverary, Argyll**

Available only from the innovative Loch Fyne Whiskies, The Living Cask is a unique recreation of a traditional Highland method of storing and serving malt whiskies. It is inspired by Professor George Saintsbury, who wrote in 1920 that the best advice is to keep a cask but not to let it empty more than half-way, and then to re-fill it up: the thinking behind the practice was that, 'the constantly changing character of the old constituents doctors the new accessions, and these in turn freshen and strengthen the old.'

THE LOCH FYNE

**Loch Fyne Whiskies,
Inverary, Argyll**

• COMMENTS •

*A malt drinker's blend,
full-flavoured with a raisiny,
sweet-spiced nose, mellow
smoothness of taste and
a warming finish. A very
easy-to-drink whisky.*

• VISITORS •

*The shop is open all year,
1000–1730 (except Sun.,
Nov.–Mar.)
Telephone 01499-302219
for mail-order information or
visit the Loch Fyne website:
www.lfw.co.uk*

Loch Fyne Whiskies is an independent specialist shop devoted to selling only whisky and whisky-related products. First registered in 1884, the current Loch Fyne blend was created by Ronnie Martin, a former production director of DCL/United Distillers. His mastery of blending was recognized when in 1996, The Loch Fyne won the bronze award in the influential International Wine & Spirit Competition. Produced in small quantities, it is available only in Argyll or by mail-order.

LOCH LOMOND

**Loch Lomond Distillers,
Alexandria, Dunbartonshire**

Loch Lomond Distillery Co. owns
three plants: one grain and two
malt, from which the components
of this whisky come. The company
is one of the newer arrivals on
the Scotch whisky scene, and also
markets the Fraser McDonald
blend. Loch Lomond also produces
a unique whisky called a single
blend: that is, a blend made from
the produce of one single company's
distilleries.

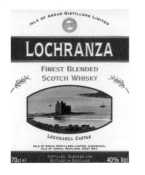

LOCHRANZA

Isle of Arran Distillers, Lochranza, Isle of Arran

40%

2

Warm and lightly sherried, this blend has fruit aromas, a sweet, oaky flavour and a light floral note on the finish with a hint of peat.

Visitors are welcome at the award-winning visitor centre. Tours are held daily. 1000–1800, mid-Mar.–end Oct. Reduced opening hours in Nov. and Dec.; telephone 01770-830264 for details.

Isle of Arran Distillers are a dynamic and independent new player in the Scotch whisky industry. Their distillery on Arran at Lochranza opened in 1995 and the company now successfully markets its portfolio of blends and malts throughout Europe, Asia and the American continent. The company's new malt, The Arran Malt, has been acclaimed by whisky writers around the world.

blend

LOCHSIDE

**Lochside Distillery,
Montrose, Angus**

● **AGE** ●

Varies

● **STRENGTH** ●

40%

● **TASTE RATING** ●

2

● **COMMENTS** ●

*A light-to-medium-bodied single
malt with a sweet, floral aroma
and drier, smooth flavour.
It is difficult to find under the
distillery label, but supplies will
continue to be available from
independent merchants.*

Established as recently as 1957,
Lochside has been one of the shorter-
lived Scotch whisky distilleries. It
was built on the site of an eighteenth-
century brewery and originally
comprised two distilleries, one grain
and one malt, as well as a blending
plant. The distillery closed its grain-
distilling and blending facilities in the
late 1970s and continued in malt
production only until 1992, when it
was shut down completely by its
Spanish owners.

single malt

LONG JOHN

**Allied Distillers,
Dumbarton, Dunbartonshire**

• AGE •
12 years

• STRENGTH •
40%, 43%

• TASTE RATING •
2–3

• COMMENTS •
*A medium-bodied blend with
a very slight peaty tang to its
pleasant, nicely rounded flavour.*

• VISITORS •
*The plant is not suitable
for visitors.*

The original company was founded by 'Long' John Macdonald, a statuesque man who built Ben Nevis Distillery at Fort William in 1825. The distillery had grain and malt stills, and its produce changed from a malt to a blend around the turn of the century. The Long John company name and the distillery went separate ways, and after passing through several hands and a company name-change to Long John International in 1971, it is now operated by Allied Distillers.

LONGMORN

**Longmorn Distillery,
Elgin, Moray**

• AGE •

15 years

• STRENGTH •

45%

• TASTE RATING •

3–4

• COMMENTS •

*Another classic Speyside malt
of great character, Longmorn
is a full-bodied whisky with a
clean, fragrant aroma and
a nutty, sweet taste.*

The distillery was built by John Duff
in 1894 and stands on the road between
Elgin and Rothes. A seventeenth-
century water wheel stands nearby,
although the distillery draws its water
from a local spring. Longmorn, along
with its sister distillery of Benriach,
merged with The Glenlivet and Glen
Grant Distilleries and Hill Thomson
to form The Glenlivet Distillers. The
distillery was known as Longmorn-
Glenlivet, but has now dropped its
hyphenated suffix. The company
is presently owned by Pernod. The
distillery is now owned by Chivas
Brothers, the Scotch whisky business
of Pernod Ricard.

LONGROW

**Springbank Distillery,
Campbeltown, Argyllshire**

• AGE •

10 years

• STRENGTH •

46%

• TASTE RATING •

5

• COMMENTS •

*Longrow is a pungent malt
whose production process, using
only peat-dried barley, lends it
a distinctive, peaty taste with
an almost medicinal aroma,
yet a complementary trace
of sweetness.*

• VISITORS •

*Springbank Distillery is open
to visitors strictly by appointment.
Telephone 01586-552085
to arrange.*

Longrow is the second single malt to be produced at Springbank Distillery. Distilled for the first time in 1973, the whisky takes its name from an old Campbeltown distillery, part of which now houses the Springbank Distillery bottling hall. Longrow is made from malt dried entirely over a peat fire and is double-distilled in the traditional Scottish manner. Like Springbank, it is neither chill-filtered nor is the colour adjusted with caramel.

single malt

MACALLAN

Macallan Distillery, Craigellachie, Banffshire

- **AGE** -

7, 10, 12, 18, 25 years

- **STRENGTH** -

40%, 43%, 57%

- **TASTE RATING** -

3–4

- **COMMENTS** -

Its rich, sherried aroma with a hint of peaches, its smooth, elegant flavour and its delightfully mellow sherry after-taste make The Macallan one of the most popular of malts.

- **VISITORS** -

There are tours and visitors are welcome 0900–1800 Mon.–Sat., Easter–Oct. Shorter hours in winter. Telephone 01340-872280.

The Macallan's distinctive richness of taste and colour derives in part from its ageing in sweet sherry casks, a traditional practice which this distillery is the only one to maintain through all its range. The distillery itself originated on a farm set above a ford over the Spey, and the first licensed distilling took place around 1824. It passed through several hands before being bought and extended in 1892 by Roderick Kemp, whose descendants owned the company until it was acquired in 1996 by Highland Distillers who were themselves taken over by the Edrington Group in 1999.

single malt

SPEYSIDE
SINGLE MALT
SCOTCH WHISKY

MORTLACH

was the first of seven
distilleries in Dufftown. In the
C19 farm animals kept in
adjoining byres were fed on
barley left over from processing.
Today water from springs in
the CONVAL HILLS is used to
produce this delightful
smooth, fruity single
MALT SCOTCH WHISKY

AGE 16 YEARS

Distilled & Bottled in SCOTLAND
DISTILLED AND BOTTLED BY
Mortlach Distillery, Dufftown, Keith, Banffshire, Scotland

43% vol   70cl

MORTLACH

**Mortlach Distillery,
Dufftown, Keith, Banffshire**

• AGE •

16 years

• STRENGTH •

43%

• TASTE RATING •

4

• COMMENTS •

*A Speyside malt of mellow,
fruity flavour with a definite
peatiness and a dryness in
the finish.*

• VISITORS •

*Visitors are welcome
by appointment.
Telephone 01340-820318
to arrange.*

Another of Dufftown's distilleries, Mortlach stands in a little valley outside the town by the River Dullan. It draws its water not from the river but from springs in the local Conval Hills. Founded in 1823, it was, in fact, the first of the distilleries to be built in the capital of Speyside whisky-making, and it enjoyed a monopoly in the town until 1887. The distillery has been modernized twice this century and is now owned by Diageo who, as United Distillers, began bottling its malt in the early '90s as part of their Distillery (Flora and Fauna) Malts series.

NORTH PORT

**North Port Distillery,
Brechin, Angus**

• AGE •

Varies

• STRENGTH •

Varies

• TASTE RATING •

2

• COMMENTS •

A sweet, fruit-syrup,
well-balanced nose and
banana flavours are followed
by a sweet finish with a slight
hint of smoke.

The older of the two distilleries in
Brechin (Glencadam being the other),
North Port was founded in 1820 by
David Guthrie, a prominent Brechin
businessman and local politician, and
managed by his sons from 1823; two
brothers in the Guthrie family had
interests in the whisky industry while
a third, Thomas, was active in the
Temperance movement. The distillery, latterly owned by the Distillers
Company Ltd, was closed down in
1983 and sold in 1990.

single malt

OBAN

**Oban Distillery,
Oban, Argyllshire**

• AGE •

14 years

• STRENGTH •

43%

• TASTE RATING •

2–3

• COMMENTS •

*An intriguing, complex malt
with a full Island character
which is balanced by a soft
Highland finish.*

• VISITORS •

*Visitors are welcome
0930–1630 Mon.–Fri., Mar.–Dec.
Weekend opening in summer
and restricted hours in winter.
Telephone 01540-677219.*

First built as a brewery in 1794,
Oban Distillery was part of the
grand plan of the Stevenson family,
energetic entrepreneurs and the
founders of modern Oban at that
time. The distillery, a grey building
standing on the harbour front,
draws its water from the Ardconnel
area of peaty uplands a mile from
the town. It is licensed to John
Hopkins, now owned by Diageo
who currently feature the single in
their Classic Malts series.

OLD FETTERCAIRN

Fettercairn Distillery, Fettercairn, Laurencekirk, Kincardineshire

First established at its present location by Sir Alexander Ramsay in 1824 and later acquired by John Gladstone, father of the great Prime Minister W.E. Gladstone, Fettercairn Distillery is situated at the edge of the Grampian Mountains, from which it takes its spring-water supplies. Despite its status as one of Scotland's oldest distilleries, it proved receptive to modern production methods when it became the first distillery in the country to use oil for heating its stills. It is presently owned by Whyte & Mackay Ltd.

OLD PARR

**United Distillers,
Banbeath, Leven, Fife**

• AGE •

12 years

• STRENGTH •

43%

• TASTE RATING •

2

• COMMENTS •

*A blend of fine whiskies,
with a smooth and mellow
taste and exceptional depth
of flavour.*

Macdonald Greenlees, the firm which first produced Old Parr, is now owned by Diageo. The whisky made its appearance in the early twentieth century, and was aimed specifically at the southern English market. After the First World War, the company amalgamated with Alexander & Macdonald of Leith and William Williams of Aberdeen, owners of Glendullan Distillery, and together they joined the Distillers Company Ltd in 1925. Old Parr is a major export blend in Central and South America, Japan and the Far East.

OLD PULTENEY

**Pulteney Distillery,
Wick, Caithness**

• AGE •
12 years

• STRENGTH •
40%

• TASTE RATING •
3–4

• COMMENTS •

*Reputedly one of the
fastest-maturing whiskies,
Old Pulteney is a distinctive
malt with a pungent aroma
and salty tang underlain by
peaty notes, perhaps due to
the exposed coastal position
of the distillery. Available from
independent bottlers.*

• VISITORS •

*Visitors are welcome:
10.30–12.30 & 13.30–15.30
Mon.–Fri., Apr.–Sept.
Oct.–Mar. by arrangement.
Telephone 01955-602371.*

Pulteney Distillery, the most northerly on the mainland, was established in 1826 in a new district of Wick which had been built to accommodate workers from the booming local herring industry, and in such a situation it had a ready market. Today, the packaging of Old Pulteney recalls the town's maritime heritage. The distillery was closed during the 1920s slump and did not reopen until 1951. It is currently owned by Inver House distillers, owners of five other malt and one grain distilleries.

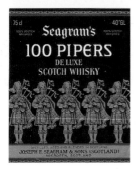

100 PIPERS

**Chivas Brothers,
Paisley, Renfrewshire**

• STRENGTH •

40%

• TASTE RATING •

2

• COMMENTS •

*A smooth, mellow blend
with a light, smoky finish.*

• VISITORS •

*The blending and
bottling plant is not open
to visitors.*

Launched in 1965, the brand name emanates from the 'Ballad of 100 pipers' celebrating Bonnie Prince Charlie's 1745 uprising when he was led into battle by a band of 100 pipers. 100 Pipers is part of Chivas Brothers portfolio, the Scotch whisky business of Pernod Ricard.

THE ORIGINAL MACKINLAY

Whyte & Mackay Ltd, Glasgow

• STRENGTH •

40%

• TASTE RATING •

2

• COMMENTS •

Delicate Speyside sweetness and light Lowland floral notes are combined with robust Highland and Island qualities to produce a blend of depth, balance and smoothness.

• VISITORS •

The blending and bottling plant is not open to visitors.

The success of the Mackinlay firm began under James, son of Charles Mackinlay, founder of the Leith company in 1824. The original Mackinlays blend appeared in 1850, and James was responsible for its success in the lucrative markets of southern England, gaining contracts to supply whisky to the House of Commons and to Ernest Shackleton's 1907 expedition to the South Pole. The company is now owned by Whyte & Mackay Ltd. As well as The Original, the Mackinlay range also includes 12-year-old and 21-year-old blends.

blend

PASSPORT

**Chivas Brothers,
Paisley, Renfrewshire**

STRENGTH
40%

TASTE RATING
2–3

COMMENTS

*A well-rounded blend
which has the Glen Keith
single malt at its core.
Sweet, slightly fruity flavours
are complemented by a
delicate, smoky finish.*

Passport is a blended Scotch with an
unusually fruity taste and a deliciously
creamy finish. Created in 1965 it
captures the essence of the Sixties era
and has Passport's strong and unusual
identity, which is particularly attractive to the target young consumer,
for whom individuality is of key importance. Passport is part of Chivas
Brothers portfolio, the Scotch whisky
business of Pernod Ricard.

PINWINNIE

**Inver House Distillers,
Moffat Distillery,
Airdrie, Lanarkshire**

• STRENGTH •

40%

• TASTE RATING •

2–3

• COMMENTS •

*A Lowland de luxe blend,
Pinwinnie is a very smooth whisky,
with sweet, fragrant notes and
a nicely rounded finish.*

• VISITORS •

*The distillery and plant is not
open to visitors.*

Pinwinnie's producers, Inver House, also own five malt distilleries: Balblair, Balmenach, Knockdhu, Pulteney and Speyburn. Blending is carried out at their complex at Moffat on the outskirts of Airdrie, which also houses a grain distillery. Pinwinnie was itself named after an area of land in the historic Monklands district, not far from Inver House head office: centuries ago the land belonged to an order of Cistercian monks from Newbattle Abbey, who were famed for their distillation skills.

PITTYVAICH

Pittyvaich-Glenlivet Distillery, Dufftown, Keith, Banffshire

Pittyvaich is a Speyside malt with a perfumed fruitiness with a hint of spice and a strong aftertaste.

A relatively short-lived distillery, built by Bell's in 1974 and now closed. The attraction in this area was the quality of its water supply, from the local Jock's Well, and the success of neighbouring Dufftown-Glenlivet Distillery almost next door. Almost all of its remaining product now goes into Diageo's blends, although some of the single malt is marketed under the distillery's own label in the Distillers (Flora and Fauna) Malts series.

PORT ELLEN

**Port Ellen Distillery,
Port Ellen, Islay, Argyllshire**

• AGE •
12 years

• STRENGTH •
40%

• TASTE RATING •
3–4

• COMMENTS •
*A medium-bodied, phenolic
malt with a smoky palate
and slightly peaty finish.*

Port Ellen was established in 1824 and
stands in the town of the same name
in the south of the island. The distillery
was closed earlier this century, from
1930 until 1967, when it was modernized and enlarged. Its produce has
been regarded by some connoisseurs
as the classic Islay malt. The distillery,
latterly owned by United Distillers
(now Diageo), has now ceased production but its malting facilities are
used by the other Islay distilleries. Port
Ellen's produce is still available from
independent bottlers.

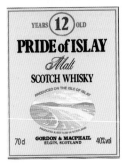

YEARS **12** OLD

PRIDE of ISLAY

Malt

SCOTCH WHISKY

PRODUCED ON THE ISLE OF ISLAY

PRODUCED & BOTTLED IN SCOTLAND

70 cl   **GORDON & MACPHAIL**
ELGIN, SCOTLAND   40%vol

PRIDE OF ISLAY

Gordon and MacPhail, Elgin, Moray

• AGE •

12 years

• STRENGTH •

40%

• TASTE RATING •

4

• COMMENTS •

One of Gordon and MacPhail's series of malts capturing the classic characteristics of the leading regions, this is a vatting of the finest whiskies produced on Islay. It has a complex nose with salty, medicinal and smoky flavours.

• VISITORS •

Gordon and MacPhail's shop, South St, Elgin is open 0900–1715 Mon., Tues. & Fri.; 0900–1700 Wed & Sat.; 0830–1715 Thurs. Telephone 01343-545110.

Gordon and MacPhail's premises are located in Elgin on the banks of the River Lossie and close to Speyside, arguably the heart of the Scotch whisky industry. The firm has been in business for over a century, initially as a licensed grocer and wine and spirit merchant. Their business encompasses the vatting, blending and bottling of whiskies, while their retail shop is among the leading malt whisky shops in the UK.

vatted malt

PRIDE OF THE LOWLANDS

**Gordon and MacPhail,
Elgin, Moray**

* AGE *

12 years

* STRENGTH *

40%

* TASTE RATING *

2

* COMMENTS *

*One of Gordon and MacPhail's
series of malts capturing the
classic characteristics of the
leading regions, this is a vatting
of the finest whiskies distilled in
the Lowlands, and has a sweet,
butterscotch-like nose with
a smoky–woody finish.*

* VISITORS *

*Gordon and MacPhail's shop,
South St, Elgin is open
0900–1715 Mon., Tues. & Fri.;
0900–1700 Wed & Sat.;
0830–1715 Thurs.
Telephone 01343-545110.*

Gordon and MacPhail started in business in 1895 as a licensed grocer and
wine and spirit merchant, as had so
many of the foremost names among
the Scotch whisky blending industry.
Unlike the others, however, Gordon
and MacPhail have retained all the
original aspects of their business as
well as extending into vatting, blending and bottling, and they are today
the world's leading malt whisky
specialists.

YEARS **12** OLD

PRIDE of ORKNEY

Highland Malt

SCOTCH WHISKY

PRODUCED IN THE ORKNEY ISLES

70 cl   Produced & Bottled in Scotland by
GORDON & MACPHAIL
ELGIN, SCOTLAND   40%vol

PRIDE OF ORKNEY

**Gordon and MacPhail,
Elgin, Moray**

• AGE •
12 years

• STRENGTH •
40%, 43%, 57%

• TASTE RATING •
3

• COMMENTS •

One of Gordon and MacPhail's series of malts capturing the classic characteristics of the leading regions, this is a vatting of the finest whiskies produced in Orkney, and is a well-balanced whisky with a sweet, toasted nose, with a hint of heather.

• VISITORS •

Gordon and MacPhail's shop, South St, Elgin is open 0900–1715 Mon., Tues. & Fri.; 0900–1700 Wed & Sat.; 0830–1715 Thurs. Telephone 01343-545110.

Gordon and MacPhail's premises are located in Elgin on the banks of the River Lossie and close to Speyside, arguably the heart of the Scotch whisky industry. The firm has been in business for over a century, initially as a licensed grocer and wine and spirit merchant. Their business encompasses the vatting, blending and bottling of whiskies, while their retail shop is among the leading malt whisky shops in the UK.

PRIDE OF STRATHSPEY

Gordon and MacPhail, Elgin, Moray

YEARS **12** OLD

PRIDE of STRATHSPEY
Highland Malt
SCOTCH WHISKY

DISTILLED IN STRATHSPEY

PRODUCED & BOTTLED IN SCOTLAND

70 cl   GORDON & MacPHAIL   40% vol
ELGIN, SCOTLAND

- **AGE** -

12, 25 years

- **STRENGTH** -

40%

- **TASTE RATING** -

2

- **COMMENTS** -

One of Gordon and MacPhail's series of malts capturing the classic characteristics of the leading regions, this is a vatting of the finest whiskies distilled in Strathspey. This malt is a citrus-fruity whisky in nose and palate, with a very pleasant aftertaste.

- **VISITORS** -

Gordon and MacPhail's shop, South St, Elgin is open 0900–1715 Mon., Tues. & Fri.; 0900–1700 Wed. & Sat.; 0830–1715 Thurs. Telephone 01343-545110.

Gordon and MacPhail started in business in 1895 as a licensed grocer and wine and spirit merchant, as had so many of the foremost names among the Scotch whisky blending industry. Unlike the others, however, Gordon and MacPhail have retained all the original aspects of their business as well as extending into vatting, blending, bottling and, more recently, distilling. They are today the world's leading malt whisky specialists.

vatted malt

ROSEBANK

**Rosebank Distillery,
Camelon, Falkirk, Stirlingshire**

• AGE •
12 years

• STRENGTH •
43%

• TASTE RATING •
2

• COMMENTS •

*One of the best known
Lowland malts, Rosebank
is a smooth, mild whisky of
light and subtle character,
which makes it ideal as a
pre-dinner dram.*

Although a distillery was operating on this site in 1817, the most recent distillery generally dates from 1840, when much rebuilding took place. Rosebank is set on the banks of the Forth and Clyde Canal on the outskirts of Falkirk. Triple-distillation processes were used at the distillery, which had one wash still and two spirit stills, giving the whisky an even smoother quality. Rosebank is now closed but the single is still available in Diageo's Distillery (Flora and Fauna) Malts series and from independent bottlers.

ROYAL BRACKLA

Royal Brackla Distillery, Cawdor, Nairnshire

HIGHLAND
SINGLE MALT *SCOTCH WHISKY*

ROYAL BRACKLA

distillery, established in 1812, lies on the *southern* shore of the MORAY FIRTH at *Cawdor near* Nairn. Woods around the *distillery* are home to the *SISKIN*; although a *shy bird*, it can often be seen *feeding* on *conifer* seeds.

In 1835 a *Royal Warrant* was granted to the *distillery* by King William IV, who enjoyed the *fresh, grassy, fruity* aroma of this *single malt whisky*.

43% vol   AGED **10** YEARS   70 cl

Bottled & Sealed in SCOTLAND. ROYAL BRACKLA DISTILLERY, Cawdor, Nairn, Scotland

William IV was known to have enjoyed Brackla's whisky and granted it his royal warrant in 1835; this was renewed by his niece, the new Queen Victoria, three years later. The queen was also known to be partial to a dram. Founded in 1812, the distillery has been rebuilt and extended several times in the past two centuries. Along with other former Dewar's distilleries, it was sold in 1998 by former owners Diageo to the Bacardi drinks group of Bermuda. However, distillery bottlings in the Distillery (Flora and Fauna) Malts livery are still available.

ROYAL LOCHNAGAR

Royal Lochnagar Distillery, Crathie, Ballater, Aberdeenshire

Lochnagar Distillery stands on the slopes of the famous mountain from which it takes its name. It was built in 1826 by James Robertson, an infamous local distiller. His line of work was not peaceful: Lochnagar was destroyed by fire, reputedly the work of rivals, in 1841 before being taken over and rebuilt by John Begg four years later. The 'Royal' prefix came after a visit and tasting in 1848 by Queen Victoria and Prince Albert who were staying at nearby Balmoral. The distillery is now owned by Diageo.

ST MAGDALENE

**St Magdalene Distillery,
Linlithgow, West Lothian**

LOWLAND MALT SCOTCH WHISKY
FROM
ST MAGDALENE
DISTILLERY

Proprietor: John Hopkins & Co. Ltd.

40%vol DISTILLED 1982 ~ BOTTLED 2001 70cl

SPECIALLY SELECTED, PRODUCED & BOTTLED BY GORDON & MACPHAIL, ELGIN, SCOTLAND

• AGE •
Varies

• STRENGTH •
40%

• TASTE RATING •
2–3

• COMMENTS •

A light-bodied Lowland malt, smooth and generally dry yet with a hint of fruity sweetness. Available only from independent merchants and their retail outlets, its produce can be difficult to find.

St Magdalene, built on the lands of St Mary's Cross towards the end of the nineteenth century, was until recently the sole survivor of the six distilleries which existed in Linlithgow in the last century. Linlithgow had been a centre of brewing and distilling due to an abundance of barley and fine water from local supplies. It was closed by its owners, United Distillers, in the mid 1980s, the building subsequently being converted to private housing.

single malt

ORCADIAN SINGLE MALT

FOUNDED 1885

SCAPA

SINGLE
ORKNEY MALT
Scotch Whisky
AGED 12 YEARS

SCAPA DISTILLERY · SCAPA FLOW · ORKNEY

40% vol   PRODUCT OF SCOTLAND   1 Litre ℮

SCAPA

Scapa Distillery, Kirkwall, Orkney

• AGE •

12 years

• STRENGTH •

40%

• TASTE RATING •

3

• COMMENTS •

Scapa, available only from independent bottlers, is a medium-bodied malt with a dryish, heathery flavour which is complemented by a satisfyingly malty sweetness.

Scapa is one of two distilleries in Kirkwall (Highland Park being the other), yet despite their proximity, their whiskies taste quite different. Scapa was built in 1885 by Macfarlane and Townsend (the latter already a well-known distiller on Speyside) and was bought by Hiram Walker in 1954. It is now owned by Allied Distillers who mothballed it in 1994. The distillery overlooks Scapa Flow where the German fleet was scuttled during the First World War.

SCOTTISH HIGHLAND LIQUEUR

The Scottish Liqueur Centre, Bankfoot, Perthshire

• AGE •
5 years

• STRENGTH •
22%

• TASTE RATING •
2

• COMMENTS •
A base of vatted malts with honey and a balancing counter-note of sloes make this an easy to drink, clear whisky liqueur.

• VISITORS •
The visitor centre welcomes visitors; telephone 01738-787044 for details.

Independent, family-owned company John Murray have been producing Columba Cream for several years to a formula which is based on a traditional recipe. As well as Murray's Scottish Highland Liqueur, the company produces Columba Cream whisky liqueur and a range of other fruit and whisky liqueurs, all made with pure ingredients and without any concentrates, flavourings, additives or GM ingredients.

SCOTTISH LEADER

Burn Stewart, Glasgow

• STRENGTH •

40%

• TASTE RATING •

2

• COMMENTS •

A smooth, well-balanced blend with honeyed flavours and mildly peaty overtones.

Scottish Leader is Burn Stewart's standard blend and complements the company's whisky portfolio which includes a range of malts from Tobermory and Deanston distilleries and two acclaimed liqueurs. Burn Stewart were themselves bought by CL Financial, an overseas company with other interests in the drinks industry, in December 2002. Several of the company's products, including Scottish Leader, have won medals in international competition.

SPEYBURN

**Speyburn-Glenlivet Distillery,
Rothes, Moray**

• AGE •
10 years

• STRENGTH •
40%

• TASTE RATING •
3–4

• COMMENTS •
*A medium-bodied whisky with
a firm yet subtle flavour and
a dry, warming, peaty finish.*

• VISITORS •
*The distillery is not open
to visitors.*

Speyburn, one of the most picturesque distilleries in Scotland, was built
in 1897 among rolling green slopes
on the outskirts of Rothes, and out-
wardly has hardly altered since then.
So keen were the proprietors to
produce a spirit in what was Queen
Victoria's Diamond Jubilee year that
the stillmen had to set to work before
doors and windows had even been
fitted. Workers wore overcoats to
protect against the cold, but the first
spirit was produced in December
1897. It was built for the blenders
John Hopkins then passed to United
Distillers before it was acquired
in 1992 by Inver House.

single malt

ESTABLISHED 1828

SPRINGBANK

Scotch Whisky

Campbeltown

SINGLE MALT

Aged 10 Years

Distilled by J & A MITCHELL & Co Ltd
Campbeltown · Scotland
PRODUCT OF SCOTLAND

70cl   46% vol

SPRINGBANK

**Springbank Distillery,
Campbeltown, Argyllshire**

• AGE •

10, 15 years

• STRENGTH •

46%

• TASTE RATING •

4

• COMMENTS •

*Often described as a classic malt,
Springbank is a smooth,
mellow whisky, light yet
complex and full-flavoured.*

• VISITORS •

*The distillery is open to visitors
strictly by appointment.
Telephone 01586-552085
to arrange.*

Springbank was built in 1828 by the Mitchell family, previous owners of an illicit still in the area. The distillery is still owned by the founders' family, and has never been closed at any time in its history. Along with Glenfiddich, Springbank is unusual in bottling on the premises, and is also the only Scottish distillery to carry out the full malt-whisky production process on site. Springbank is not coloured with caramel, and is one of the only malts available under a distillery label which has not been chill filtered. Longrow single malt is also produced here.

STAG'S BREATH LIQUEUR

Meikles of Scotland, Newtonmore, Inverness-shire

• STRENGTH •

19.8%

• TASTE RATING •

2

• COMMENTS •

A light and smooth union of fine Speyside whisky with fermented comb honey. Equally suited to a role as an aperitif or as a digestif.

Meikles of Scotland is a small Speyside family firm and has been producing Stag's Breath since 1989. The liqueur takes its name from one of the fictional whiskies lost at sea in Sir Compton Mackenzie's famous re-telling of the sinking of the *SS Politician*, in his book, *Whisky Galore*.

EST 1831

RARE SELECTED
STEWARTS
CREAM OF THE
BARLEY
BLENDED SCOTCH WHISKY

DISTILLED BLENDED & BOTTLED IN SCOTLAND
STEWART & SON OF DUNDEE LIMITED
DUNDEE SCOTLAND
100% SCOTCH WHISKIES
40% vol   70 cl

STEWART'S CREAM OF THE BARLEY

Allied Distillers, Dumbarton, Dunbartonshire

STRENGTH

40%

TASTE RATING

2

COMMENTS

A popular and good-quality blend with a soft and well-balanced, sweetish, malty flavour.

VISITORS

The plant is not suitable for visitors.

Stewart & Son of Dundee was founded in 1831 and was one of the first companies to exploit newer methods of distilling (particularly the new patent still) and the beginnings of the market for blended whiskies. The company grew steadily in size and the brand in popularity. It was bought by Allied-Lyons in 1969 and today operates under Allied Distillers as one of their most popular standard blends for the UK market.

STRATHISLA

**Strathisla Distillery,
Keith, Banffshire**

• AGE •
12 years

• STRENGTH •
43%

• TASTE RATING •
4

• COMMENTS •
*A big, robust whisky which is
full-flavoured and fruity, with
a nutty, sherried sweetness.*

• VISITORS •
*Visitors are welcome
1000–1600 Mon.–Sat.,
1230–1600 Sun.
Admission £5 (under 18s free).
Apr.–Oct. inclusive.
Telephone 01542-783044.*

Strathisla distillery is the oldest working distillery in the Scottish highlands, which lies on the bank of the river Isla. Its prized malt whisky is a key ingredient in Chivas Regal 12 Years Old. Strathisla is owned by Chivas Brothers, the Scotch whisky business of Pernod Ricard.

single malt

ISLE OF SKYE

TALISKER

SINGLE MALT SCOTCH WHISKY

45.8% vol   TALISKER DISTILLERY CARBOST SKYE   1 Litre

**Talisker Distillery,
Carbost, Isle of Skye,
Inverness-shire**

• AGE •

8, 10 years

• STRENGTH •

45.8%

• TASTE RATING •

5

• COMMENTS •

*Talisker is Skye's only malt
and has been described as
being mid-way between
Islay and Highland malts.
It is full-bodied with a rich,
peaty flavour and elements
of malty, fruity sweetness.*

• VISITORS •

*Visitors are welcome
0930–1630 Mon.–Fri.,
Apr.–Oct.,
and by appointment
1400–1630 Nov.– Mar.
Also open Sat., July–Sept.
Telephone 01478-614308.*

Talisker Distillery had an inauspicious start in the 1830s, being denounced by a local minister as a great curse for the area. Despite his disapproval, distilling has continued successfully, with the distillery changing hands several times. A victim of several fires throughout its 160-year history, it was totally rebuilt in 1960. The distillery is owned today by Diageo, and some of its product goes into Johnnie Walker blends. The malt was praised by Robert Louis Stevenson in his poem, *The Scotsman's Return from Abroad*, as one of 'The king o' drinks'.

TAMDHU

**Tamdhu Distillery,
Knockando, Aberlour,
Banffshire**

• AGE •

No age given

• STRENGTH •

40%, 43%

• TASTE RATING •

3

• COMMENTS •

*A good, light-to-medium
Speyside malt, which is slightly
peaty but with a delicate
sweetness and a long,
subtle finish.*

• VISITORS •

*The distillery is not open
to visitors.*

Highland Distilleries bought this distillery shortly after it opened in 1897 and have owned it ever since. It was extensively refurbished in the 1970s and is now one of the most modern distilleries on Speyside. Tamdhu once used the hyphenated Glenlivet suffix, but this has been dropped in recent years. As well as its appearance as a single malt, Tamdhu features in the Famous Grouse blend, owned by the Highland subsidiary Matthew Gloag & Son.

single malt

TAMNAVULIN

**Tamnavulin Distillery,
Tomnavoulin, Banffshire**

<table>
<tr><td>• AGE •</td></tr>
<tr><td>10 years</td></tr>
</table>

<table>
<tr><td>• STRENGTH •</td></tr>
<tr><td>40%</td></tr>
</table>

<table>
<tr><td>• TASTE RATING •</td></tr>
<tr><td>3</td></tr>
</table>

<table>
<tr><td>• COMMENTS •</td></tr>
</table>

*A lightish, mellow Glenlivet-
type malt with a sweetish
bouquet and taste but
an underlying grapey note.*

Opened in 1966, this was one of the
newest Highland distilleries. A rather
functional building, it is set on slopes
above the River Livet and used water
from a nearby burn. This is another
distillery which once carried the
hyphenated Glenlivet suffix but has
since shed it. Tamnavulin was owned
until 1993 by Invergordon Distillers,
but Whyte & Mackay acquired it that
year, mothballed production and
closed the visitor centre. In 2001 a
management buy-out saw it pass to
new group, rather confusingly named,
Whyte & Mackay Ltd, but the distillery remains mothballed.

TEACHER'S HIGHLAND CREAM

Allied Distillers, Dumbarton, Dunbartonshire

• STRENGTH •

40%, 43%

• TASTE RATING •

2

• COMMENTS •

Teacher's Highland Cream is a superior blend which has a smooth, sweet flavour with a trace of drier, heathery notes. It has a particularly high malt content of 45%. Its sister blend is the 12-year-old Teacher's Royal Highland.

• VISITORS •

The plant is not suitable for visitors.

The Teacher's company was begun in Glasgow in the 1830s by William Teacher, a young man barely in his twenties. It started with licensed premises where people could drink whisky, and expanded to include blending, bottling and export interests. Highland Cream was first marketed in 1884, although Teacher's did not build its first distillery, at Ardmore, until 1898. The company has since concentrated on blending, bottling and exporting, selling off its licensed shops. Today Allied Distillers own the blend and sell more than 1.5 million cases of it in 150 countries.

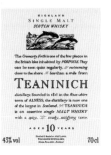

HIGHLAND
SINGLE MALT
SCOTCH WHISKY

The *Cromarty Firth* is one of the few places in
the British Isles inhabited by *PORPOISE*. They
can be seen quite regularly, *swimming*
close to the shore. *less than a mile* from

TEANINICH

distillery. Founded in 1817 in the *Ross-shire*
town of ALNESS, the *distillery* is now one
of the largest in *Scotland*. TEANINICH
is an assertive *single* MALT WHISKY
with a *spicy, smoky, satisfying* taste.

AGED 10 YEARS

43% vol   70cl

Teaninich Distillery dates from the
early 1800s and in 1887 it was
recorded as the only distillery north
of Inverness to be 'lighted by electricity'. The majority of the present
buildings date from the 1970s and
it is now owned by Diageo who,
as United Distillers, reopened it in
the '90s after several years in mothballs. Most of the production has
traditionally gone into blending,
but the single malt has become
easier to find since its official
bottling as part of Diageo's Distillery (Flora
and Fauna) Malts series.

TEANINICH

**Teaninich Distillery,
Alness, Ross-shire**

• AGE •
10 years

• STRENGTH •
43%

• TASTE RATING •
3

• COMMENTS •
*Teaninich is an assertive
whisky with a spicy, smoky
and wholly satisfying taste.*

• VISITORS •
*Visitors are welcome
by appointment only.
Telephone 01349-882461
to arrange.*

TOBERMORY

**Tobermory Distillery,
Tobermory, Mull, Argyllshire**

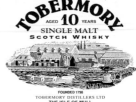

AGED **10** YEARS
SINGLE MALT
SCOTCH WHISKY

FOUNDED 1798
TOBERMORY DISTILLERS LTD
THE ISLE OF MULL
PRODUCT OF SCOTLAND

• AGE •
10 years

• STRENGTH •
40%

• TASTE RATING •
3

• COMMENTS •
*A nicely balanced, light malt
with a delicate, flowery
aroma and drier, spicy,
heathery tones in its flavour.
A good pre-dinner dram.*

• VISITORS •
*The Visitor Centre and
Distillery Shop are open
Mon.–Fri., Easter–30 Sept.
Tours can be arranged at
other times in the year.
Telephone 01688-302645.*

Set in a wooded site by the sea,
Tobermory Distillery has enjoyed
mixed fortunes since it was first established in 1823. It has been closed
several times during its existence,
most recently in the 1980s when
it was mothballed. Having reopened
in 1990, the distillery is now back in
production. The distillery was previously known as Ledaig but changed
its name in the 1970s; a single malt
marketed under the old name is
available. Tobermory was bought by
Burn Stewart Distillers in 1993.

single malt

TOMATIN

**Tomatin Distillery,
Tomatin, Inverness-shire**

• AGE •

10, 12, 25 years

• STRENGTH •

40%, 43%

• TASTE RATING •

2

• COMMENTS •

*A lightly peated and delicately
flavoured malt which makes
a pleasant aperitif.*

• VISITORS •

*Visitors are welcome
0900–1700 (last tour 1530)
Mon.–Fri., all year, and
0900–1300 Sat.
(last tour 1200), May–Sept.
Large parties must book
in advance.
Telephone 01808-511444.*

At over 1000' above sea level, Tomatin
is one of Scotland's highest distilleries.
Situated in the Monadhliath Mountains
from where it draws its water supply,
the distillery was established in 1897
on a site famed for whisky distilling
since the sixteenth century. A major
programme of expansion in the early
1970s made Tomatin the largest
distillery in Scotland. The company
suffered its share of the industry down-
turn in the 1980s and was eventually
bought by a Japanese consortium,
so making it the first Scotch whisky
distillery to have Japanese owners.

TOMINTOUL

**Tomintoul Distillery,
Ballindalloch, Banffshire**

Built in 1964 near to Tomintoul, the
second-highest village in Scotland
and once a centre for illicit distilling,
Tomintoul distillery is also, at 1100',
one of the highest in the country.
It draws its water from the nearby
Ballantruan Spring. Tomintoul's owners in the past decade have included
Invergordon Distillers and Whyte &
Mackay but the distillery is currently
owned by Angus Dundee.

THE TORMORE

**The Tormore Distillery,
Advie, Grantown-on-Spey,
Moray**

This was Speyside's first new distillery built in the twentieth century. Built in 1959, it is not traditional looking but is an attractive complex in a pleasant Highland setting. The distillery has the delightfully kitsch touch of a chiming clock which plays the air *Highland Laddie* every hour. Tormore's water comes from the Achvochkie Burn, fed by the nearby Loch an Oir (Lake of Gold). The distillery itself is owned by Allied Distillers who feature its produce in their Long John blends. Allied also produce a Tormore 12 Year Old single Speyside malt, The Pearl of Speyside.

• AGE •
12 years

• STRENGTH •
40%, 43%

• TASTE RATING •
2–3

• COMMENTS •
A medium-bodied whisky, rich and slightly nutty in flavour. An after-dinner dram.

• VISITORS •
Visitors are welcome by appointment 1330–1600 Mon.–Thurs., June–Sept. Telephone 01807-510244 to arrange.

TULLIBARDINE

**Tullibardine Distillery,
Blackford, Perthshire**

• AGE •

Varies

• STRENGTH •

40%

• TASTE RATING •

2–3

• COMMENTS •

*Tullibardine is a good,
all-round single malt,
smooth and mellow with
a fruity flavour giving it
a special roundness.*

Tullibardine Distillery was built on the site of a medieval brewery reputed to have produced ale for the coronation of James IV in 1488. It was opened as a distillery in 1949 and is actually situated at Blackford, a few miles away from Tullibardine village. The distillery was bought from Whyte & Mackay Ltd in 2003 by a small private company. It has been recommissioned and although new stock will not be ready until 2013, maturing stock ensures supplies of Tullibardine will not run out. The new owners also plan to open a state-of-the-art visitor facility in August 2004.

single malt

VAT 69

**Diageo,
Kilmarnock, Ayrshire**

• STRENGTH •

40%

• TASTE RATING •

3

• COMMENTS •

*A smooth, well-balanced
and distinctly mature blend,
light but with a pleasantly
malty background.*

William Sanderson was a Leith wine and spirit merchant who moved into whisky blending in the 1860s. Keen to find a notable blend to market, he produced 100 different whiskies to be tested, each in a numbered cask. The unanimous choice of his associates was the whisky from vat number 69, and so the name suggested itself. William Sanderson's son was responsible for advertising and marketing successes after the new blend's launch in 1882. Today Sanderson and its brands are owned by Diageo.

WALLACE

**The Wallace Malt Liqueur Co.,
Deanston, Perthshire**

WALLACE
Single Malt
SCOTCH WHISKY
LIQUEUR

*A combination of Deanston's
single malt, fruit and herbs,
this rich liqueur has a delicate
texture with a hint of honey.*

This relative newcomer made an
immediate impact on the Scotch
liqueur market after its launch. It is
named after Sir William Wallace,
Guardian of Scotland. His famous
victory in 1297 over the English at
the battle of Stirling Bridge took
place only a few miles from
Deanston Distillery, whose malt is
a major component of the liqueur.
Originally a cotton mill dating from
1785, Deanston was converted to
a distillery in 1966 and draws its
waters from the nearby River Teith.
Deanston was bought by Burn
Stewart of Glasgow in 1991.

liqueur

WHITE HORSE

**Diageo,
Glasgow**

• STRENGTH •

40%

• TASTE RATING •

2–3

• COMMENTS •

*White Horse is a smooth
and distinctive whisky with
peaty elements in both
its aroma and flavour.
It is the leading standard
blend in Japan.*

White Horse Distillers, known until 1924 as Mackie & Co., was established by James Logan Mackie in 1861, but its real successes came under its entrepreneurial second owner, Peter Mackie. He registered the 'White Horse' name, after a famous Edinburgh coaching inn, in 1890, and by the time he died in 1924 his whisky was one of the world's foremost blends. White Horse also produce Logan and White Horse Extra Fine de luxe blends for the export market. The company is today owned by Diageo.

blend

WHYTE & MACKAY SPECIAL RESERVE

Whyte & Mackay Ltd, Glasgow

• STRENGTH •

40%

• TASTE RATING •

2

• COMMENTS •

A good quality, smooth, light-bodied whisky with a well-rounded, mellow sweetness which is said to come from the particular blending process the company uses.

Whisky merchants James Whyte and Charles Mackay began their partnership and blending firm in 1882. The company expanded steadily, mainly through the strength of overseas markets, for the next century, merging with Dalmore Distillery, with whom it had had a long-standing relationship, in the 1960s. Fettercairn and Tomintoul-Glenlivet distilleries followed in 1972, with another four malt and one grain distilleries coming with the acquisition of Invergordon Distillers in 1993. The company was subject to a management buy-out in 2001.

APPENDICES

Appendix 1:
INDEX OF MALT WHISKIES BY PRODUCING REGION

malts by region

Appendix 2: MINIATURES

The following lists all the whiskies featured in this book and their current availability as miniatures (although not necessarily produced by the distillery). Information about miniatures can be obtained from The Mini Bottle Club (see p. 55).

A

Aberfeldy	Yes
Aberlour	Yes
Allt-a-Bhainne	Yes
An Cnoc	Yes
The Antiquary	Yes
Ardbeg	Yes
Ardmore	Yes
The Arran Malt	Yes
Auchentoshan	Yes
Auchroisk (formerly Singleton of Auchroisk)	No
Aultmore	No*

B

The Bailie Nicol Jarvie	Yes
Balblair	Yes
Ballantine's Finest	Yes
Balmenach	Yes
The Balvenie	Yes
Banff	Yes
Bell's Extra Special	Yes
Ben Nevis	Yes
Benriach	Yes
Benrinnes	Yes
Benromach	Yes
Big "T"	Yes
Black & White	Yes
Black Bottle	Yes
Bladnoch	Yes
Blair Athol	Yes
Bowmore	Yes
Brora	Yes
Bruichladdich	Yes
Bunnahabhain	Yes

C

Cameron Brig	No*
Caol Ila	Yes
Caperdonich	Yes
Cardhu	Yes
Chivas Regal	Yes
The Claymore	Yes
Clynelish	Yes
Columba Cream	Yes
Convalmore	Yes
Cragganmore	Yes
Craigellachie	Yes
Crawford's Three Star	Yes
Cutty Sark	Yes

D

Dailuaine	Yes
Dallas Dhu	Yes
The Dalmore	Yes
Dalwhinnie	Yes
Deanston	Yes
Dewar's White Label	Yes
Dimple	Yes
Drambuie	Yes
Drumgray Highland Cream Liqueur	Yes
Dufftown	Yes
Dunhill Old Master	Yes
Dunkeld Atholl Brose	Yes

E

Edradour	Yes

F

Fairlie's Light Highland Liqueur	Yes
The Famous Grouse	Yes
Fraser MacDonald	Yes †

G

Glayva	Yes
Glenburgie	Yes
Glencadam	Yes
Glen Calder	Yes
Glen Deveron	Yes
Glendronach	Yes
Glendullan	Yes
Glenfarclas	Yes
Glenfiddich	Yes
Glen Garioch	Yes
Glengoyne	Yes
Glen Grant	Yes
Glen Keith	Yes
Glenkinchie	Yes

The Glenlivet	Yes	Inchgower	Yes
Glenlochy	Yes	Inchmurrin	Yes
Glenlossie	Yes	Inverleven	Yes
Glen Mhor	Yes	Islay Mist	Yes
Glenmorangie	Yes	Isle of Jura	Yes
Glen Moray	Yes	Isle of Skye	Yes
Glen Ord	Yes		
Glen Rosa	Yes	**J**	
The Glenrothes	Yes	J&B Rare	Yes
Glen Scotia	Yes	Johnnie Walker	
Glentauchers	Yes	Black Label	Yes
The Glenturret	Yes	Johnnie Walker	
The Glenturret		Blue Label	No*
Original Malt Liqueur	Yes	Johnnie Walker	
Glenury Royal	Yes	Red Label	Yes
Grand MacNish	Yes		
William Grant's		**K**	
Family Reserve	Yes	Knockando	Yes
H		**L**	
Haig	Yes	Lagavulin	Yes
Heather Cream	Yes	Langs Supreme	
Highland Park	Yes	Laphroaig	Yes
		Lauder's Scotch	Yes
I		Ledaig	Yes
Immortal Memory	Yes	Linkwood	Yes
Imperial	Yes	Littlemill	Yes

The Living Cask	No	Pittyvaich	Yes
The Loch Fyne	Yes	Port Ellen	Yes
Loch Lomond	Yes	Pride of Islay	Yes
Lochranza	Yes	Pride of the Lowlands	Yes
Lochside	Yes	Pride of Orkney	Yes
Long John	Yes	Pride of Strathspey	Yes
Longmorn	Yes		
Longrow	Yes	**R**	
		Rosebank	Yes
M		Royal Brackla	Yes
The Macallan	Yes	Royal Lochnagar	Yes
Mortlach	Yes		
		S	
N		St Magdalene	Yes
North Port	Yes	Scapa	Yes
		Scottish Highland	
O		Liqueur	Yes
Oban	Yes	Scottish Leader	Yes
Old Fettercairn	Yes	Speyburn	Yes
Old Parr	Yes	Springbank	Yes
Old Pulteney	Yes	Stag's Breath Liqueur	Yes
One Hundred Pipers	Yes	Stewart's Cream	
The Original Mackinlay	Yes	of the Barley	Yes
		Strathisla	Yes
P			
Passport	Yes	**T**	
Pinwinnie	Yes	Talisker	Yes

miniatures

Tamdhu	Yes	**V**	
Tamnavulin	Yes	VAT 69	Yes
Teacher's			
Highland Cream	Yes	**W**	
Teaninich	Yes	Wallace	Yes
Tobermory	Yes	White Horse	Yes
Tomatin	Yes	Whyte & Mackay	
Tomintoul	Yes	Special Reserve	Yes
The Tormore	Yes		
Tullibardine	Yes		

* These were available from the distillers as give-aways and so are
not readily available to the general public.

† available mainly in Italy.

Appendix 3:
FURTHER INFORMATION

On the web

There are many whisky-related websites out there, and possibly the best way to find them is to type 'Scotch whisky' into a search engine such as Google (**www.google.com**), and investigate what comes back. The following are particularly useful.

The Scotch Whisky Association (**www.scotch-whisky.org.uk**) has a comprehensive selection of links on its site to producers, distilleries, retailers, publications, organisations and tours.

whisky.com is a site with extensive coverage of whisky-related events taking place around the world.

www.maltwhiskytrail.com tells you everything you need to know if you're planning a trip to one – or all – of the Speyside distilleries and cooperage that particularly welcome visitors.

Finally, if you're planning on visiting the Scottish distilleries from inside the UK or from outside the country, tourism site **www.visitscotland.com** can help with general and visitor information.

Reading

Possibly the best whisky book available for both the beginner and experienced whisky drinker is Phillip Hills' *Appreciating Whisky* (HarperCollins, Glasgow). All the whisky-related information you need is in this book but most interesting of all is possibly the author's tutoring on how to develop the palate – leaving readers to find out which whiskies they actually prefer, rather than simply going by a whisky reviewer's opinion. The book was called in one review, 'Independent-minded, witty, erudite and on occasion iconoclastic or downright bawdy'.

So, something for everyone.